OCTOBER 03 2006

Rick,

WE APPECIATE EVUS &
WE'RE THANKFULL TO ' , WORK
WITH YOU.

ENJOY YOU'RE RETIREMENT, YOU DESERVE IT!

THE SHIPS OF CANADA'S MARINE SERVICES

THE SHIPS OF

CANADA'S

MARINE SERVICES

CHARLES D. MAGINLEY AND BERNARD COLLIN

Vanwell Publishing Limited

St. Catharines, Ontario

Vanwell Publishing acknowledges the financial support of the Government of Canada through the Book Publishing Industry Development Program for our publishing activities.

Design: Linda Moroz-Irvine
Front cover: Painting of N.B. McLean by Yves Bérubé
Back cover: Painting of Diana by Yves Bérubé

Vanwell Publishing Limited
1 Northrup Crescent
P.O. Box 2131
St. Catharines, Ontario L2R 7S2
sales@vanwell.com
phone 905-937-3100
fax 905-937-1760

Printed in Canada

Canadian Cataloguing in Publication Data

Maginley, Charles D. (Charles Douglas), 1929-
    The ships of Canada's marine services

Includes bibliographical references and index.
ISBN 1-55125-070-5

  1. Ships–Canada–History. I. Collin, Bernard, 1955-   II. Title.

VM26.M33 2001   623.8'26'0971   C2001-902008-2

CONTENTS

Foreword(s) VII

Acknowledgements IX

Preface X

Notes on the statistical information XI

Part 1   1850-1945   Introduction 13
Chapter 1   Pre-Confederation general duties vessels 17
Chapter 2   Northern exploration ships 25
Chapter 3   Icebreakers 33
Chapter 4   Lighthouse supply vessels and buoy tenders 45
Chapter 5   Customs and RCMP patrol vessels 69
Chapter 6   Fisheries patrol vessels 81
Chapter 7   Hydrographic survey ships 92
Chapter 8   Miscellaneous vessels 105

Part 2   1946-2000   Introduction 117
Chapter 9   The Eastern Arctic patrol ship 145
Chapter 10   Postwar icebreakers 147
Chapter 11   The cable ship 159
Chapter 12   Weather ships 161
Chapter 13   Navigation aids vessels 165
Chapter 14   Special river navigation aids tenders 192
Chapter 15   Northern supply vessels 199
Chapter 16   Search and rescue cutters 203
Chapter 17   The RCMP Marine Division 213
Chapter 18   Postwar fisheries patrol vessels 219
Chapter 19   Fisheries research vessels 230
Chapter 20   Hydrographic and oceanographic ships 239
Chapter 21   Naval Auxiliary vessels 255
Chapter 22   Postwar miscellaneous vessels 269
Chapter 23   Hovercraft 277

Index of ships 281

List of Sources 287

The Authors 288

Dedicated to the crews of the Canadian Government ships that have performed essential services to the Nation and to mariners, Canadian and foreign, for 150 years.

FOREWORD

FOR MANY YEARS, CANADIAN VESSELS and their many services have positively impacted the people of this country and helped shape our maritime heritage. Fisheries and Oceans has had a long-standing role in the formation and development of this country's civilian fleet, so it is with great pleasure that I write an introduction to this book, which celebrates the fleet's history and achievements.

In 1867, the federal government's role in civilian marine services began with the formation of the Department of Marine and Fisheries, which evolved over time to become what is now known as Fisheries and Oceans Canada. The Canadian Coast Guard, meanwhile, was introduced in 1962, replacing the Canadian Marine Service fleet of the Department of Transport and eventually merging with Fisheries and Oceans Canada in 1995. While the names and, indeed, the scope and nature of the services provided by Canada's civilian fleet might have changed somewhat in the intervening years, its role has remained constant. Search and rescue, flood control, meteorological data, marine research, law enforcement and patrol services are just a few of the services the government has provided, and continues to provide today, to support our country's economic, ecological, and scientific interests.

This book—a comprehensive exploration of the foremost civilian vessels that have proudly served Canadians for 150 years—fills a long-standing gap in the records of the Canadian Coast Guard and the Department of Fisheries and Oceans. As a relatively new member of the Department, I find the information contained within its pages to be quite valuable. Its directness and simplicity—complemented by close to 350 high-resolution photos of these diligent and celebrated vessels—make it an appealing and constructive resource for all Canadians.

I'd like to compliment both authors on the excellent work they have undertaken in the creation of this book. Bernard Collin, currently working at Canadian Coast Guard headquarters in Ottawa, processed the images, electronically restoring many old and rare photographs, some from as early as 1850. The accompanying technical and historical documentation, written by former Canadian Coast Guard College instructor Charles Maginley, add to the interesting illustrations and make for a fascinating read.

This book is a useful tool and should serve as an ample reminder to Canadians of the important role the government and marine services have played in shaping this country and its history.

Wayne G. Wouters
Deputy Minister
Fisheries and Oceans Canada

FOREWORD

CANADA'S HISTORY is manifestly linked to the sea. Early explorers, traders and settlers traversed our oceans and inland waterways in their search for new lands and new opportunities, and many made their living from the ocean's bounty. Their exploits were not without hazards, however, and as a maritime nation Canada has always lived up to its obligation to make its seas and waterways as safe as possible, a tradition that lives on today in the work of the Canadian Coast Guard.

While the title "Canadian Coast Guard" was introduced in 1962, many of the services we provide have been around since well before the days of Confederation. Be it the buoy tender marking hazards for others to avoid; the search and rescue vessel patrolling the waters, or the icebreaker leading trade to Canada's ports through all four seasons, the vessels of the Canadian Coast Guard and its predecessor organizations have been a familiar and welcome sight to Canadians for more than 200 years.

This book provides a detailed history of the many vessels that have impacted the lives of Canadians. It is a testament to the accomplishments of both the Canadian government and, more specifically, the individuals who have served to make this country a leader in marine safety and environmental response. It provides detailed descriptions of important ships, lifeboats and hovercraft, as well as the people who crewed them, and offers a fascinating glimpse into the evolution of vessels over time, and the advances of marine technology that have made such evolution possible.

Both authors have invested countless hours researching and assembling this book in order to preserve the long history of the Canadian Coast Guard and its ancestor organizations, and both are eminently qualified to serve as archivists of the Canadian Marine Services' proud heritage. Bernard Collin has extensive experience as a Coast Guard ship radio officer and at Coast Guard headquarters, while Charles Maginley—following a career in the Merchant Service and the Canadian Navy—was a long-time instructor at the Canadian Coast Guard College. Their skills and knowledge are complementary, and only their combined input could make a book like this possible.

I am pleased to see a book like this make its way into publication. As Coast Guard sets its course for the future, this important work will help remind Canadians of the already formidable contribution the ships of the Canadian Marine Services have made to this country's proud history.

John Adams
Commissioner
Canadian Coast Guard

ACKNOWLEDGEMENTS

WE WOULD LIKE TO THANK the following people who, either in a professional capacity or because of their personal interest and knowledge, have contributed to the success of this work.

Special thanks for their contribution and continuous support to our wives, June and Danièle, Stephen Peck, Peter Ballard and Ginette Dion from the Canadian Coast Guard Fleet HQ in Ottawa.

For their artistic contribution we are grateful to Yves Bérubé, Lunenburg, NS; F.R. Berchem, Newmarket, ON; and Robin Wyllie, East La Have, NS.

The following individuals and organizations have provided invaluable information and expertise: Margaret Evans, Royal Canadian Mounted Police; Carmen Harry, RCMP Museum, Regina; Marc Milner, University of New Brunswick, Moncton; Lynn-Marie Richard, Maritime Museum of the Atlantic, Halifax; Marilyn Gurney, Maritime Command Museum, Halifax; William P. Moran, Oshawa; Henny Nixon, Ottawa; Rollie Webb, Seattle, Washington; Boyde Beck, Charlottetown; and Dr. David J. McDougall, Lachine.

We would like to thank the following institutions for graciously permitting us to use photographs from their collections: Fisheries and Oceans Canada; National Archives of Canada; Department of National Defence, Ottawa; Department of National Defence Photographic Unit, Halifax; Royal Canadian Mounted Police, Ottawa; Royal Canadian Mounted Police Museum, Regina; British Columbia Archives; Vancouver Maritime Museum; Nova Scotia Archives; Maritime Museum of the Atlantic, Halifax; Maritime Command Museum, Halifax; Prince Edward Island Museum, Charlottetown; The Confederation Centre Art Gallery, Charlottetown; the North West Territory Archives; and the McCord Museum of Montreal.

The following individuals have contributed photographs from their own collections, Ron Beaupré, Port Elgin; Yves Bérubé, Lunenburg; M. B. Mackay, Halifax; Ken Macpherson, Port Hope; Phillip Murdock, Ottawa; and Captain Earle Wagner, Halifax.

PREFACE

CANADA PROBABLY HAS THE MOST CHALLENGING conditions for seafarers of any country in the world. No nation has a longer coastline. The climate is severe and navigation is often made hazardous by ice, fog and storm, while the Arctic Regions are only navigable for part of the year with the support of specially strengthened vessels. The sea always has and always will take its toll of the unwary and the unlucky, but the governments of nations with maritime interests will endeavour to make their seas and waterways as safe as possible by providing aids to navigation, including, in Canada's case, icebreaker support, and by helping ships in difficulty or distress. Of equal importance is the need to regulate and protect resources such as the fisheries and, in recent years, underwater petroleum and mineral reserves.

To survey and mark our coasts and waters, and to maintain the lighthouses and floating aids, specialized vessels are needed. Icebreakers are required to assist shipping and prevent flooding. Fishing regulations must be enforced by patrol craft, while in later years an offshore search and rescue organization has been developed in addition to station-based lifeboats. All these tasks require the Government of Canada to provide and operate a considerable fleet of ships and small craft of widely different design and purpose. Some are impressive by reason of their size, power or unique design. Others are unglamorous work horses that, nevertheless, are engaged in tasks that are essential to the safety of mariners.

The purpose of this book is to record and illustrate the historic, hard working ships that have helped shape our history and our maritime heritage. These are the civilian-crewed vessels owned and operated by the Canadian Coast Guard and its predecessors: the Marine Service of the Department of Transport, the Department of Fisheries, the Hydrographic Service and the original Department of Marine and Fisheries. Also listed are the vessels of the Customs Preventive Service, the patrol vessels of the RCMP and those the Canadian Naval Auxiliary Service. It does not include vessels owned by the Department of Public Works and by the St. Lawrence Seaway authority.

In order to keep the book's size within reasonable limits, it is restricted, for the most part, to vessels of 100 gross registered tons or greater. However, a few craft under this arbitrary size are too important to be omitted, especially the search and rescue cutters and lifeboats that have often been in the public eye. Hovercraft, the first of which entered service in 1968, are also included. Part 1 of the book includes vessels built or purchased between 1849 and 1945 and mentions a few earlier vessels of some significance. Part 2 describes those built or acquired between 1946 and 2000.

NOTES ON THE STATISTICAL INFORMATION

THE DATES FOLLOWING EACH SHIP'S NAME are the years during which the ship served in the fleet of a civil Department of the Government of Canada.

The tonnage of the ships in this book is, for the most part, given in gross registered tons. This is not a measure of weight but represents the total internal volume of a ship in measurement tons of 100 cu.ft, with certain spaces exempted. Net registered tons, used very occasionally, is obtained by deducting from gross registered tons the volume reserved for machinery and crew accommodation spaces. The term "tons burden" applying to a few of the very earliest ships was an arbitrary measurement system that became obsolete in the mid-nineteenth century. For Naval Auxiliary Vessels, the measure used is tons displacement.

The length, breadth and draft are given in feet for ships in both parts of the book and also in metres for ships in Part 2. When draft is not available, depth is given. (Draft is the distance between the waterline and the keel, with the ship in normal condition. Depth is the distance from the main deck to the floors or the top of the keel).

The only available power measurement for many older ships is nominal horsepower (NHP), sometimes given as rated horsepower (RHP). This is based on the cross-sectional area of the cylinders and takes no account of improvements in efficiency that accrued with developments in engineering. It was essentially for regulatory and tax purposes and was retained in registry and reference books for far too long.

The power of ships with steam reciprocating engines is given, when available, in indicated horsepower (IHP). This is an actual measurement of the engine's output derived from the pressure in the cylinders, their dimensions and the revolutions per minute.

The power of motor ships is given in brake horsepower (BHP), which takes into account the internal friction of the engine. It is so called because it was originally measured by a device resembling a brake, but nowadays is found by using a dynamometer.

The power of steam and gas turbine ships and of ships with turbo-electric or diesel-electric drive is given in shaft horsepower (SHP). This is the power that reaches the propeller shaft after losses in the gearing or, in the case of electric drive, in the generators and electric motors, are accounted for.

IHP, BHP and SHP (but not NHP or RHP) can also be expressed in kilowatts (kW). (One HP = 746 watts). The rating in kW, which is the current method of expressing power, is given for later vessels and for older ships still in service.

The normal full speed of ships is given when known. This is seldom available from earlier registers and reference books.

Numbers in brackets after a name: (1), (2), (3), indicate the first, second or third ship of that name in Canadian government service during the period covered by this book.

As this book deals almost exclusively with Canadian government ships, it has seldom been necessary to use the abbreviations that normally precede a ship's name. For ships in this book these would be CGS for Canadian Government Ship, CGSS for Canadian Government Survey Ship and CCGS for Canadian Coast Guard Ship. The prefix for warships is HMCS for His (or Her) Majesty's Canadian Ship and CNAV for Canadian Naval Auxiliary Vessel.

A Note on Photographs

All the photographs featured in this book have been electronically modified for greater clarity.

The abbreviations in the photo credit lines indicate the following Institutions : DFO, Fisheries and Oceans Canada; NAC, National Archives of Canada; DND, Department of National Defense (Ottawa); MCM, Maritime Command Museum (Halifax); RCMP, Royal Canadian Mounted Police (Ottawa); CCAGM, Confederation Centre Art Gallery and Museum (Charlottetown); MMM, McCord Museum of Canadian History (Montreal); MMA, Maritime Museum of the Atlantic (Halifax); VMM, Vancouver Maritime Museum; PEIPA, Prince Edward Island Public Archives; BCA, British Columbia Archives.

PART 1 1850–1945

INTRODUCTION

THE CIVILIAN-CREWED FLEET of the Government of Canada came into being at the time of the confederation of the four provinces of Ontario, Quebec, New Brunswick and Nova Scotia on 1 July 1867. A Department of Fisheries and Marine was constituted at the outset and the Act formally authorizing it as a legal entity was passed on 22 May 1868 at the first session of the Dominion Parliament. Among the responsibilities assigned to the Department by this Act was the "operation of steamers and vessels belonging to the Government of Canada, except gunboats or other vessels of war." The Department's fleet was initially composed of vessels inherited from the various pre-confederation colonial administrations.

The types of vessel best suited to the various tasks of a government fleet are not large in comparison to contemporary commercial vessels, but all those ordered by the Dominion Government were built to the highest standards extant at that time. A succession of ships, each an improvement on the last, put Canada in the forefront of icebreaker development and, by the early years of the twentieth century, an optimum design for lighthouse and buoy tenders had evolved which is still evident in the latest ships of this type. Patrol craft, originally like the fishing vessels they policed, came to look like miniature warships, then reverted to fishing trawler design. Hydrographic vessels, painted white, had the

13

appearance of contemporary steam yachts and were decorated with bow scrolls and coats of arms. The long service life of so many of these Canadian government ships attests not only to their superior construction but to conscientious maintenance by their crews.

The fleet, however, has not always been operated and administered by one department. Between 1884 and 1995 branches were formed, ministries were divided, rejoined and were renamed, and responsibility for different programs and services were shifted from one department to another. These rather bewildering bureaucratic and administrative dances are best shown in chronological form.

Administrative changes up to 1945

1868	Department of Marine and Fisheries instituted.
1884	Marine and Fisheries become separate Departments.
1892	Marine and Fisheries re-united and given responsibility for hydrography and tidal survey.
1897	The Preventive Service of the Department of Customs and Excise assumes control of Customs vessels already in service.
1904	St. Lawrence ship channel responsibilities transferred to Marine and Fisheries from the Department of Public Works. The Canadian Hydrographic Survey is officially established.
1910	Hydrography, tidal survey and wireless telegraphy transferred to the newly formed Department of Naval Service.
1914	Fisheries patrol and the lifeboat service transferred to the Department of Naval Service, now the Royal Canadian Navy.
1920	Fisheries patrol and the lifeboat service returned to Marine and Fisheries.
1922	Hydrography, tidal survey and wireless telegraphy returned to Marine and Fisheries.
1927	Marine and Fisheries become separate branches.
1930	Marine and Fisheries again become separate Departments.
1932	The Marine Section of the RCMP is formed and takes over the fleet of the Customs Preventive Service.

1936	The Department of Transport is formed and takes over the Department of Marine fleet, except for the Hydrographic Service and its vessels which go to the Department of Mines and Resources.
1939	The ships and personnel of the RCMP Marine Section are incorporated into the Royal Canadian Navy and the RCAF. Most of the hydrographic survey and fisheries patrol vessels are taken over by the RCN for use as patrol craft, training ships or gate vessels. Department of Transport ships continue their regular work under wartime conditions, but icebreakers are employed on missions to new bases in Labrador and the Arctic.
1946	The requisitioned ships that are still serviceable are returned to their original departments.

(Changes after the Second World War are shown in the Introduction to Part 2)

Colour schemes of ships in Part 1

The earliest iron steamers were painted black and had black smokestacks. Deckhouses and superstructures, usually wood, were white or varnished. Wooden vessels, especially the smaller ones, sometimes had white hulls. The larger Marine and Fisheries ships later had black hulls, white bulwarks and superstructures, buff masts and buff funnels with a black top, while smaller wooden vessels continued to use white on the hull, especially on the Great Lakes. Early West Coast ships had a plain buff or yellow funnel. In the early 1930s, gray hulls and yellow funnels made their appearance but in 1936 the Department of Transport reverted to the original black, white and buff livery. From the 1890s, hydrographic ships were painted white with yellow funnels and masts, as were ships used as government yachts like the *Earl Grey* and *Lady Grey*. The *Canada* was also painted white for training cruises to the Caribbean. When warships changed their colour scheme to overall gray in the early years of the last century, the fisheries patrol vessels followed suit. During both world wars ships of all types were gray, sometimes retaining a black funnel top. Unlike naval ships, civilian vessels did not adopt multi-coloured camouflage paint schemes.

CHAPTER 1

PRE-CONFEDERATION GENERAL DUTIES VESSELS

In the days before icebreaking was a practical proposition, the efforts of the colonial governments to aid mariners were confined to the provision of lighthouses and some floating navigation aids. The area which was the most difficult to navigate and which had, by mid-century, an increasing volume of traffic, was the St. Lawrence River. Sailing ships had to contend with the shoals and river currents and could only go upstream with the tide. The limit of navigation for large seagoing ships was Lac St. Pierre. To make navigation safer, the government of the Province of Canada, (united in 1841 as recommended by the Durham Report), formed the Quebec and Montreal Trinity Houses, (the name taken from the venerable institution that administered the English navigation aids). These organizations found it convenient to put the work out to contract and the main contractor was François Bâby. He was already managing the paddle steamer *Doris* for the Quebec Trinity House when he obtained a contract, issued by the Department of Public Works, "to establish and maintain a line of Steam Tug Boats to run between Quebec and Bic for the purpose of aiding vessels and relieving wrecks, when directed". In addition, the work of these vessels included lighthouse supply, buoy tending and sometimes a passenger service. This arrangement went into effect in February 1854. Mr. Bâby used two wooden river paddle steamers, the *Admiral* and *Advance*, in addition to the *Doris*, but soon ordered four iron vessels to be built in Scotland. The two largest were the *Queen Victoria* and the *Napoleon III*, named for the reigning sovereigns of England and France. The others were the *Druid* and the *Lady Head*. Just before his contract ran out in 1860, these ships were purchased by the government and the survivors, together with the *Richelieu*, formed the basis of the fleet of the Department of Marine and Fisheries when the Dominion of Canada came into being on 1 July 1867.

In 1864 the Government of the Colony of British Columbia ordered a small screw steamer to assist the dredges and barges that were deepening Victoria harbour. When the work was completed, the *Sir James Douglas* continued to be busily employed on a variety of tasks, including towing, lighthouse supply and transporting government officials.

RICHELIEU 1849-1880

Built:	Montreal, QC
Date Completed:	1845
Tonnage:	126 (gross)
Dimensions:	130 x 18 x 7 (depth) (ft)
Machinery:	Steam sidewheeler, 20 NHP

An iron hulled paddle steamer, built in 1845 and purchased by the Montreal Trinity House in 1849 as a tug, lighthouse supply and buoy vessel to work between Montreal and Sorel. Not only is this little ship the oldest steamer featured in this book, she was the longest lasting, being finally scrapped in 1958. The *Richelieu* sank after a collision off Trois Rivières in 1877, but was raised and repaired. She was transferred from Marine and Fisheries to the Harbour Commissioners for Montreal in 1880 and sold to a private buyer in 1883. In 1893 she was rebuilt, with tonnage reduced to 113. She was again rebuilt in 1902 and the tonnage increased to 167, probably by additions to the superstructure, as the dimensions remained the same. Boilers and machinery would have been replaced during one or other of these rebuilds but she remained a sidewheel paddler to the end. She appears to have been used as an excursion vessel and the photograph above, from an old postcard, was taken at the turn of the century and shows a summer cruise with the ladies in white dresses and stylish hats. The destination is probably an American port upriver from Montreal, as the stars and stripes is at the masthead and Canadian ensigns fore and aft. In 1906 she was renamed *Beauharnois* and she passed through a series of different owners, mostly in the Beauharnois, Valleyfield and Coteau du Lac area where she was used as a ferry. By 1939 she belonged to the Cie des Traversiers at Valleyfield and received a final rebuild in 1941 with a tonnage change to 129. She was retired in 1954 and broken up in 1958 when she was 113 years old.

DORIS 1850-1855

Built:	Cork, Ireland
Date Completed:	1846
Tonnage:	223 (gross)
Dimensions:	142 x 21 x 13 (ft)
Machinery:	Steam sidewheeler

A wooden paddle steamer, purchased in 1850 as a fisheries patrol vessel but proved unsatisfactory. Subsequently managed by F. Bâby, under contract to the Quebec Trinity House, as a lighthouse supply and buoy vessel. Sold 1855. Wrecked 1856.

Admiral. DFO

ADMIRAL 1854-1861

Builder:	Niagara Harbour and Dock Co, ON
Date Completed:	1854
Tonnage:	289 (gross)
Dimensions:	155 x 20 x 8.5 (ft)
Machinery:	Steam walking-beam sidewheeler, 72 NHP

A wooden paddle steamer used in the St. Lawrence for towing, pilotage duties, buoy work and for transferring immigrants from deep sea ships. The *Admiral* was owned by F. Bâby who was contracted by the Quebec Trinity House to provide these services. The photos show that she was a typical river paddle steamer. Purchased by the government in 1860 but sold (commercial) 1861 and rebuilt as a schooner.

ADVANCE 1854-1868

Builder:	Wilson, Quebec City, QC
Date Completed:	1853
Tonnage:	393 (gross)
Dimensions:	164 x 26 x 8 (ft)
Machinery:	Steam walking beam sidewheeler, 90 NHP

A wooden paddle steamer, used in the St. Lawrence for towing, pilotage duties, buoy work and general duties along with the *Admiral* and *Doris*. No photo has been found but she was similar in appearance to the *Admiral*. Purchased from F. Bâby in 1860. Sold (commercial) 1868. Wrecked 1872.

QUEEN VICTORIA 1856-1866
NAPOLEON III 1856-1890

Builder:	Robert Napier, Glasgow
Date Completed:	1856
Tonnage:	495 (gross)
Dimensions:	173 x 30 x 16 (ft)
Machinery:	Single screw steam, two-cylinder, oscillating, (geared), 300 NHP, replaced in *Napoleon III in* 1887 with a compound engine.
Speed:	13 kts

Iron screw steamers, ordered from Napier by François Bâby and owned by him until 1860, when they were purchased by the Commissioner of Public Works. Used for towing sailing vessels, lighthouse supply, buoy handling and general duties on the St. Lawrence River and Gulf.

In 1864 the *Queen Victoria* took the "Fathers of Confederation" to Charlottetown, PEI, for the conference that resulted, three years later, in the creation of the Dominion of Canada. In 1866 the ship was chartered to a commercial company for a voyage to Cuba. On the return voyage she encountered a hurricane and received damage that resulted in her foundering off Cape Hatteras. The American brig *Ponvert* was able to rescue most of the crew and passengers and the *Queen Victoria*'s bell is now in the museum at Prospect Harbour, Maine, the brig's home port.

Napoleon III. Sketch by Marine Artist Robin H. Wyllie

The *Napoleon III* was identical to the *Queen Victoria*. Both ships had additional plating at the bow for two feet above and below the waterline as strengthening against ice. In 1887 the *Napoleon III* was fitted with the boilers and engines taken from the wrecked steamer *Fylgia* and continued in service until 18 October 1890, when she was wrecked at Little Glace Bay.

The 1856 painting of the *Napoleon III,* reproduced here, shows the ship in what may have been her original configuration although some artistic license may be involved. Later photographs show a bridge at the forward end of the superstructure and no bowsprit, as in the large model on display at Confederation Centre in Prince Edward Island.

DRUID (1) 1856-1901

Builder:	Todd and M'Gregor, Glasgow
Date Completed:	1856
Tonnage:	239 (gross)
Dimensions:	160 x 21 x 7.5 (ft)
Machinery:	Steam sidewheeler; 2 steeple engines, 170 NHP

Converted in 1894 to single screw steam compound.

An iron paddle steamer used as a lighthouse tender, buoy vessel and on fisheries protection duties in Nova Scotia. In 1868 she grounded, incurring considerable damage. After repair, she was transferred to the St. Lawrence, exchanging duties with *Lady Head*. The *Druid* was used on several occasions to take governors general on tours of the lower provinces. In 1878 she brought the Marquess of Lorne and his wife, Princess Louise, to Charlottetown, PEI. During their visit, the Vice-regal couple declined to move to Government House, as the ship was more comfortable and, furthermore, had flush toilets, which Government House lacked! The *Druid* was re-engined and converted to screw in 1894. Sold in 1901, she remained in commercial service on the Great Lakes until 1936.

LADY HEAD 1857-1878

Builder:	Robert Napier, Glasgow
Date Completed:	1857
Tonnage:	299 (gross)
Dimensions:	151 x 24 x 13 (ft)
Machinery:	Single screw, steam oscillating, 150 NHP

An iron screw steamer purchased from F. Bâby in 1860. The ship was named for the wife of Sir Edmund Head, Governor-in-Chief of the United Provinces of Upper and Lower Canada. Used on passenger service between Quebec and New Brunswick and subsequently as a lighthouse supply vessel and buoy tender in the Maritimes. Wrecked at Pte. Jaune, Gaspé, in August 1878.

Sir James Douglas. DFO

SIR JAMES DOUGLAS (1) 1864-1899

Built:	Victoria, BC
Date Completed:	1864
Tonnage:	153 (gross)
Dimensions:	116 x 19 x 10.5 (ft)
Machinery:	single screw steam, 40 NHP

A wooden screw steamer named for the Province's first governor, the "Father of British Columbia." Built by the government of British Columbia as a tugboat to move dredgers and barges in Victoria harbour, she was soon employed taking officials along the east coast of Vancouver Island, on fisheries patrol and as a lighthouse supply and buoy vessel. In 1883 she was lengthened by 20 feet. In 1890, on the arrival of the new steamer *Quadra*, she was retired but occasionally used as a relief vessel. She was not sold until 1899 and eventually broken up 1900.

CHAPTER 2

NORTHERN EXPLORATION VESSELS

In 1880 the British Government transferred sovereignty over the Arctic archipelago to Canada. Until then, exploration of the Region had been conducted by the British and Americans and much of what had been charted was a result of the many expeditions in search of Sir John Franklin and his crew. Yet Ottawa showed little interest in the far north—the Government was far more concerned with the route through Hudson Strait to the western shores of Hudson Bay, for it was already foreseen that a railway line must eventually reach a Hudson Bay port. In 1884 the Newfoundland sealing vessel *Neptune* was chartered for an expedition under Lt. Andrew Robertson Gordon. In the following year the *Alert,* a former Royal Navy sloop that had been specially converted for Arctic service, was acquired from the Royal Navy and used for two voyages in 1885 and 1886. As a result of these three expeditions, Lt. Gordon recommended Churchill as the railway terminal, although nearly fifty years would elapse before the tracks would arrive there.

In 1897, the Dominion government chartered the Newfoundland-owned whaling ship *Diana* for an expedition to the Hudson Strait under Dr. William Wakeham, to conduct geological, fisheries and ice surveys; but the first attempt to establish an official Canadian government presence in the higher latitudes of the Eastern Arctic was not made until 1903, when the *Neptune* was again chartered. She was commanded by Captain S.W. Bartlett, who had sailed with US Admiral Robert Peary in 1898 on one of his earlier attempts to reach the North Pole. The officer in charge was Dr. A.P. Low of the Geological

Survey. Major Moodie of the Northwest Mounted Police and a detachment of police accompanied Low on this voyage. The *Neptune* wintered in Chesterfield Inlet in Hudson Bay and in 1904 continued up Davis Strait and Baffin Bay to Cape Herschell on Ellesmere Island where a cairn was erected and the sovereignty of the crown in right of Canada was proclaimed. On her return voyage, the *Neptune* met the *Arctic* (Captain J.E. Bernier), on the first of many expeditions providing a Canadian government presence in the high Arctic. The *Arctic* would spend the winter in harbours such as Pond Inlet and Arctic Bay on northern Baffin Island while dogsled expeditions continued the work of survey and exploration. On July 1, 1909 Captain Bernier erected a plaque at Winter Harbour on Melville Island to "commemorate the taking possession for the Dominion of Canada of the whole Arctic archipelago lying to the north of America...to Latitude 40°N."

In 1913, the Vilhjalmur Stefanson expedition to the western Arctic started out in a former salmon packer, the *Karluk*. Stefanson landed in Alaska to continue his journey but the ship was crushed in the ice in January 1914. By his unrelenting determination and almost superhuman endurance her commander, Captain Robert A. Bartlett, managed to effect the rescue of his crew. His feat is considered to be among the finest episodes in Canadian maritime history.

The last of the wooden ships to patrol the Arctic was the RCMP vessel *St. Roch*. From 1928 this vessel and her detachment of Mounties were the principal representatives of the Canadian government in the western Arctic. When war was declared in 1939 Commissioner Wood, who had first seen the need for an RCMP patrol vessel, ordered Staff Sergeant Henry Larsen, the Captain of the *St. Roch*, to take the ship through the Northwest Passage to Halifax as a demonstration of Canadian sovereignty in the North. In 1940 the passage was blocked and the ship continued on routine duties. In 1941 they reached the Boothia Peninsula and wintered there, conducting long patrols by dog sled. In 1942, they broke through and arrived at Halifax in October of that year. In 1944, again under Henry Larsen, the *St. Roch* returned to Vancouver by a more northerly route, Prince of Wales Strait. This was done in a single season and the ship arrived in Vancouver in October 1944. The *St. Roch* was the first ship to make a west to east transit of the Northwest Passage and the first to make the transit in both directions.

All of these ships were built of wood and while they were immensely strong, they were designed to survive in ice, not to smash through it. They had auxiliary sails and small engines that needed only modest amounts of fuel and were capable of carrying stores and food for two or more years. Wooden vessels had another advantage over iron ships. They were less likely to be affected by compass deviation in areas near the magnetic pole where the directive force is weaker. They were also more comfortable for the crew than the iron vessels of the day because of better insulation and less condensation.

NEPTUNE   Chartered 1884-1885 and 1903-1904

Builder:	Alexander Stephen and Sons, Dundee, Scotland
Date Completed:	1872
Tonnage:	684 (gross)
Dimensions:	190 x 30 x 18 (depth) (ft)
Machinery:	Single screw steam compound, 110 NHP
Speed:	9 kts

A wooden, schooner-rigged Newfoundland sealer, she was chartered in 1884 for a survey expedition to Hudson Bay under Lt. Andrew R. Gordon (later Commander of the Fisheries Protection fleet 1891-93) and reached York Factory and Churchill. In 1885 she was used to assist the *Northern Light* on the Prince Edward Island service but was ineffective. In 1903-1904 she was again chartered for an expedition under Dr. A.P. Low which established and proclaimed Canadian sovereignty in the north. The first photo shows the *Neptune* in winter quarters at Fullerton, Hudson Bay, in 1904. In her later years the *Neptune*

lost her mainmast and acquired a midship deckhouse, a modern bridge and a tall funnel. She continued in the seal hunt and as a coastal freighter until she sank near St. John's in 1943.

ALERT (1) 1885-1895

Builder:	Royal Dockyard, Pembroke, Wales
Date Completed:	1856
Tonnage:	700 (gross)
Dimensions:	160 x 36 x 16.5 (ft)
Machinery:	Single screw steam compound, 60 NHP
Speed:	8.5 kts

A wooden, barquentine rigged naval sloop. In 1874 she was converted for Arctic exploration (the Nares expedition of 1875). She was re-engined, strengthened with iron above the waterline and sheathed overall with various types of wood. In 1876 the ship reached Lat. 82°N and crew members on a dogsled expedition attained 83°20.5'N, a record at that time. In 1884 the *Alert* was lent to the United States Navy for the successful rescue of the Greely expedition. In 1885 she was acquired, on loan, by the Canadian Department of Marine to continue the *Neptune's* survey work in Hudson Bay (Lt. Gordon). From 1887 to 1894, with a cut-down rig, she served

as a lighthouse supply vessel and buoy tender. Sold for breaking up in 1895. The first photo was taken in the Arctic during the 1885 expedition. The second shows her during her lighthouse and buoy tending years.

DIANA Chartered 1897

Builder:	Alexander Stephen and Sons, Dundee, Scotland
Date Completed:	1871
Rebuilt:	1891
Tonnage:	291 NRT
Dimensions:	151 x 24 x 16.6 (depth) (ft)
Machinery:	Single screw steam compound

A typical barquentine rigged Dundee whaler and sealer built for Job Bros. St. John's Newfoundland as the *Hector*. She was rebuilt in 1891 and renamed *Diana*. Chartered by the Canadian government in 1897 for an expedition to the Hudson Strait area, under Dr. William Wakeham, to conduct geological, fisheries and ice surveys. The *Diana* was crushed in the ice in 1922 while engaged in the annual seal hunt.

Arctic. NAC PA207089

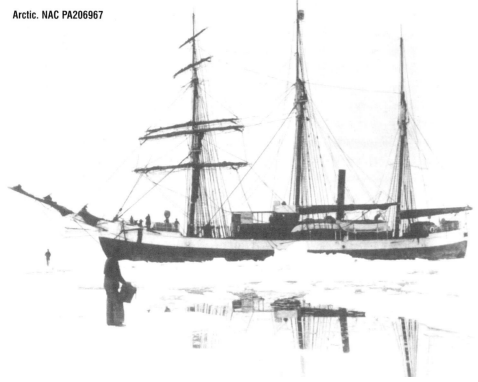

Arctic. NAC PA206967

ARCTIC 1904-1926

Builder:	Howaldtswerke, Kiel, Germany
Date Completed:	1901
Tonnage:	762 (gross)
Dimensions:	165 x 37 x 20 (depth) (ft)
Machinery:	Single screw steam triple expansion, 44 NHP
Speed:	8 kts

The *Arctic* was constructed as the German Antarctic expedition ship *Gauss*. She was built of wood with a hull shape modeled on Nansen's ship *Fram*—that is, if beset in ice, she would be squeezed upward rather than crushed. The *Arctic* had a low-powered engine and was rigged as a barquentine. She was purchased by the Canadian government in 1904 as an Arctic patrol vessel and was commanded by Captain Joseph Eléazar Bernier who had surveyed her and recommended her purchase. Captain Bernier and the *Arctic* made annual expeditions to the north, often wintering over and returning south the following year. During the First World War Bernier commanded transatlantic ships, but in 1922-1925 rejoined the *Arctic* for her annual northern patrol. The ship was now old and worn out and her commander elderly. The *Arctic* was sold and broken up in 1926. The photographs show her in a typical Arctic scene and under full sail. Captain Bernier passed away in 1934. He is considered to be Canada's pre-eminent Arctic sailor.

The annual patrols were continued by ice-strengthened merchant vessels, first the *Beothic*, and the *Ungava*, chartered from Job Brothers of St. John's, Newfoundland, and then the Hudson Bay Company's *Nascopie*. (See Chapter 8)

Karluk. BCA HP075540

Karluk. DFO

KARLUK 1913-1914

Built:	Benicia, CA
Date Completed:	1884
Tonnage:	321 (gross)
Dimensions:	126 x 27 (ft)
Machinery:	Single screw steam compound

A wooden vessel built as a salmon carrier from Alaska to California. Strengthened for service in ice, but not to the standard of the other ships described in this chapter. Rigged as brigantine.

In 1913 the Canadian explorer Vilhjalmur Stefanson planned a western Arctic expedition to see if there was a major landmass north of Alaska and the Beaufort Sea. It was to be financed by the National Geographic magazine and the expedition ship would be commanded by Captain Robert A. Bartlett, a Newfoundlander and an experienced Arctic hand who had commanded Peary's ship *Roosevelt* in expeditions in 1905-1909. Bob Bartlett was the nephew of Captain Sam Bartlett of the *Neptune*.

Realizing that any land discovered might come under Canadian sovereignty, the government took over the financing of the expedition and prepared the expedition ship, the *Karluk*, in Esquimalt naval dockyard. The *Karluk's* service as a Canadian government ship would be short-lived. She was caught fast in the ice off the coast of Alaska and Stefanson and his party landed to commence what would become a five-year journey through the Arctic Regions. The ship was driven westward in the grip of the ice and on 11 January 1914 was finally crushed and sank. Captain Bartlett led the ship's company across the ice to Wrangell Island and then continued with one Inuit companion 110 miles across the ice to Siberia, then south on the coast of Asia until he was able to take ship to Alaska. The United States Coast Guard cutter *Bear* was put at his disposal and he proceeded to Wrangell Island to rescue his crew, but the B*ear* was delayed by its normal duties and by ice and it was the small walrus-hunting schooner *King & Winge* which found twelve survivors in September 1914 and transferred them to the *Bear*. Eleven others had died: four who had elected to try for the coast of Alaska when the ship sank, four whose bodies were later found on Herald Island and three of Bartlett's party who died on Wrangell. Captain Bartlett is rightly recognised as a Canadian hero.

RCMP St Roch. VMM

St Roch. NAC PA121409

ST. ROCH 1928-1954

Builder:	Burrard Drydock, North Vancouver, BC
Date Completed:	1928
Tonnage:	193 (gross)
Dimensions:	104 x 24.75 x 13 (ft)
Machinery:	Single screw diesel 150 BHP
	As re-engined in 1944: Single screw diesel 300 BHP
Speed:	8 kts

The *St. Roch* was a wooden auxiliary schooner, designed by Charles Duguid, the naval constructor for the Department of Marine and Fisheries. She was built as an Arctic patrol vessel for the RCMP. After her 1928-29 maiden voyage, the ship normally remained in the Arctic during the winter while police patrols were conducted by dog sled. She returned to Vancouver only when refits were needed: in 1934 and 1937. In 1939 at the outbreak of war, she was recalled but in 1940 to 1942 under her long time commander, Staff Sergeant Henry Larsen, she made the first west to east transit of the Northwest Passage. In 1943 she made a supply trip to Baffin Island and then was modified for a return passage through the Arctic. She was fitted with a more powerful engine and a larger deckhouse and her sailing rig was much reduced. In 1944 she made the east to west transit of the Northwest Passage in one season, using a more northerly route. In 1948 she was retired, but in 1950 Larsen sailed her to Halifax via the Panama Canal, making her the first ship to circumnavigate North America. In 1954 she returned to Vancouver for preservation as a museum vessel. Restored to her original configuration, she was placed ashore in 1958 and incorporated into the Vancouver Maritime Museum in 1960. In 1965-66 the previous restoration work was reversed: she was once again altered to the arrangements made for the 1944 westward passage. The first photo shows the vessel in her original configuration and the second as modified for the return journey in 1944.

CHAPTER 3
ICEBREAKERS

The early icebreakers, built for the purpose, can be divided into two groups: those intended primarily for maintaining a winter passenger link with Prince Edward Island and those acquired to combat spring flooding in the St. Lawrence River and expedite the opening of the navigation season.

Although the Charlottetown Conference in 1864 paved the way for Confederation, the small colony of Prince Edward Island did not join with Canada until 1873 and then only under certain conditions: the construction of a railway on the island and the provision of a winter passenger and goods service by steam vessels. The first of these winter ferries was the unsatisfactory *Northern Light* of 1876, but she was followed by superior icebreakers, the *Stanley*, the *Minto* and the magnificent *Earl Grey*.

The St. Lawrence River vessels were the *Montcalm* and the smaller *Champlain* and *Lady Grey*. On her first season, the *Montcalm* was considered a marvel, cutting a broad channel through thick ice and releasing enormous quantities of water, preventing the usual flooding. It was found that two vessels working together gave the best results, with the larger icebreaker working in mid-channel and a smaller vessel widening the lead and working in confined areas.

In the summer and fall, commercial vessels took over the PEI link and the icebreakers were used for lighthouse supply and other duties. They also participated in missions to Hudson Bay. In the First World War, three Canadian icebreakers were sold to the Russian government (the old *Montcalm* went there in the Second World War). From 1917, icebreaking commercial ferries were able to take over the PEI link year-round.

In the inter-war period two larger icebreakers, *Mikula*, (ex *J.D. Hazen*) and *N.B. McLean* and the smaller *Saurel,* were the mainstays of the fleet. Another smaller ship, the *Ernest Lapointe,* was completed in 1941.

Northern Light. Harper's Weekly

Northern Light. Canadian Illustrated News

NORTHERN LIGHT 1876-1890

Builder:	E.W. Sewell, Lévis, QC
Date Completed:	1876
Tonnage:	393 (gross)
Dimensions:	144 x 25 x 16 (depth) (ft)
Machinery:	Single screw steam compound, 120 NHP
Speed:	14kts, (doubtful)

According to the terms under which Prince Edward Island joined confederation in 1873, the Dominion government was obliged to provide a winter communication service with the mainland. Efficient summer steam ferry service was already available but when the Strait of Northumberland was frozen, open boats carrying passengers and mail and traveling in threes were dragged over the ice or rowed through open leads. It was three years before a pioneer icebreaker, *Northern Light,* was completed. She was strongly built of wood and had a rounded midship section, not unlike modern icebreakers, and a reverse rake or ram bow. Speed in open water was supposed to be 14 knots and it was intended that she should tow ships through ice, but in practice she was often unable to cope with conditions, occasionally being frozen in for several weeks with passengers on board. When this occurred it was necessary to revert to the system of open boats. In 1887 she was assisted by the *Neptune* and later by the *Lansdowne,* but both were too underpowered to be effective. She was replaced by the *Stanley* in 1888 and sold in 1890.

STANLEY 1888-1935

Builder:	Fairfield Shipbuilding and Engineering, Glasgow
Date Completed:	1888
Tonnage:	914 (gross)
Dimensions:	207 x 32 x 13.5 (ft)
Machinery:	Single screw, steam triple expansion, 2300 IHP
Speed:	15 kts

The Canadian government's first effective icebreaker was developed from Danish and Swedish designs for Baltic ice steamers. The *Stanley* was a successful and long lasting steel vessel. She provided the winter ferry service to Prince Edward Island and was certified to carry passengers. Like her predecessor *Northern* Light, she was sometimes unable to cope with conditions and was occasionally stuck in mid-passage. (Even large modern icebreaking ferries can find themselves in the same predicament.) In the spring and fall the *Stanley* was used as a lighthouse supply and buoy vessel and in summer on fisheries patrol. In 1910 she sailed to Hudson Strait and Hudson Bay in company with the *Earl Grey,* to survey the route to Churchill and Port Nelson. She returned to that area in 1912. In 1927 she accompanied the *Montcalm* and a chartered freighter on another expedition to Hudson Bay, where the railway to Churchill was being completed. The *Stanley*, named for the Governor-General of the day, was a handsome ship with a clipper bow and a small bowsprit. The second of the two photos shows her with two sailing vessels in the La Have River near Bridgewater. The *Stanley* gave 47 years of faithful service and was retired in 1935 and scrapped in 1936.

Stanley. DFO

Stanley. DFO

Minto. PEIPA 2301/285

MINTO 1899-1915

Builder:	Gourlay Bros., Dundee, Scotland
Date Completed:	1899
Tonnage:	1089 (gross)
Dimensions:	225 x 32.5 x 20.5 (depth) (ft)
Machinery:	Single screw, steam triple expansion, 2900 IHP
Speed:	16 kts

A steel icebreaker, named for the Governor-General, the Earl of Minto. She was somewhat larger and more powerful than the *Stanley* and had a rounded bow without a bowsprit. She was used on the Prince Edward Island passenger service in winter and for lighthouse supply and buoy work during other seasons. In 1911, 1912 and 1915, she carried out survey work in Hudson Bay. During the First World War, the Russians, who needed icebreakers to keep traffic moving in their northern ports, purchased the *Minto*. In November 1915 under the command of Captain John Read, she sailed for Arkangel'sk. On arriving in the White Sea she spent several weeks breaking British and Russian vessels out of the ice. Captain Read escorted coal-laden vessels to those short of

Minto. MMA

bunkers and gave food to many ships that had exhausted their provisions. In this she was assisted, not very effectively, by the *Kanada*, formerly the *Earl Grey*. The *Minto* was eventually handed over to a Russian crew and the Canadians were taken ashore by horse and sled. The *Minto* had several changes of name in Russian and Soviet hands. She was the *Ivan Susanin* when she was wrecked in 1922.

The first photo appears to show the ship as newly completed.

MONTCALM (1) 1904-1942

Builder:	Fleming and Ferguson, Paisley, Scotland
Date Completed:	1904
Tonnage:	1432 (gross)
Dimensions:	252 x 41 x 19 (depth) (ft)
Machinery:	Twin screw steam triple expansion, 3600 IHP
Speed:	14 kts

Montcalm. Ken Macpherson (Private Collection)

The *Montcalm* was intended for service in the St. Lawrence to clear ice jams, thereby preventing flooding in the spring, and to escort shipping. In the summer and fall she was engaged in lighthouse supply and made several northern voyages, including the 1927 Hudson Bay expedition. In 1941 she was presented to the Soviet Union and followed the route of her former sister ships during the First World War. The *Montcalm* was unwelcome in a convoy because of the smoke from her old coal fired boilers. In 1942, on her third attempt (under Captain F.S. Slocome, nor-

mally examiner of Masters and Mates at Toronto), she reached Murmansk and was handed over to the Soviet authorities. Believed broken up postwar.

CHAMPLAIN 1904-1920

Builder: Fleming and Ferguson, Paisley, Scotland
Date Completed: 1904
Tonnage: 522 (gross)
Dimensions: 132 x 30 x 11 (depth) (ft)
Machinery: Single screw steam triple expansion, 1850 IHP
Speed: 13 kts

A smaller icebreaker designed to work with the *Montcalm* in the St. Lawrence. As the larger ship cut the main channel, the smaller icebreaker would widen it and clear the mouths of the tributaries and the smaller ports. The *Champlain* was sold in 1920. She was lost off Newfoundland in January 1943.

Lady Grey. DFO

Lady Grey. DFO

LADY GREY 1906-1955

Builder:	Vickers, Sons and Maxim, Barrow-in-Furness, England
Date Completed:	1906
Tonnage:	733 (gross) (824 (gross) after 1943 rebuild)
Dimensions:	183.5 x 32 x 12 (ft)
Machinery:	Twin screw steam triple expansion, 2300 IHP
Speed:	14 kts

Another small icebreaker for St. Lawrence service. She had good accommodation and was often used to take officials on inspection tours. The first photo shows her in her original configuration. The *Lady Grey* was rebuilt at Montreal in 1943 and emerged completely changed in appearance, as shown in the second photo, with better buoy handling capability. In February

1955 she was attempting to help the Quebec to Lévis ferry in ice conditions when a collision occurred. The *Lady Grey* sank and was a total loss.

EARL GREY 1909-1914

Builder:	Vickers, Sons & Maxim, Barrow-in-Furness, England
Date Completed:	1909
Tonnage:	2357 (gross)
Dimensions:	250 x 48 x 24 (ft)
Machinery:	Twin screw steam triple expansion, 6000 IHP
Speed:	17 kts

Earl Grey. MMA MP28.32.4

This beautiful, well-appointed and powerful ship named for the popular Governor-General was designed by Charles Duguid, chief naval architect for the Department of Marine and Fisheries, and built for the Prince Edward Island winter passenger service. Her profile, with a clipper bow and bowsprit, resembled the luxurious steam yachts of the era while her appointments and passenger accommodation equaled the best commercial passenger vessels. On several occasions she acted as the Vice-regal yacht, taking the Governor-General on some of his visits to remoter parts of the Dominion. In 1910 the *Earl Grey* and *Stanley* surveyed the Hudson Bay route to Churchill. Earl Grey and his entourage had traveled to York Factory by canoe and joined the ship for the voyage through Hudson Strait and south. On the outbreak of war in August 1914, a Russian delegation visited and expressed interest in acquiring the *Lady Grey* to help keep the port of Arkangel'sk open, but when a formal request came it was for the *Earl Grey*, possibly a mistake. However, an agreement was reached and in 1915 she temporarily became HMCS *Earl Grey* and was taken to Murmansk by Captain Charles Trousdale, RN, and a naval crew. She was renamed *Kanada* by the Imperial Russian Navy and after the Revolution she became the *Fedor Litke* and for many years gave excellent service. In 1934 she made the first transit of the Northern Sea Route in a single season. After the Second World War she was used for scientific work in the Siberian Arctic and as late as 1955 she reached 83°11' North Latitude, 409 miles from the Pole. She was broken up in 1959 and her wheelhouse is preserved at the maritime museum in Moscow. The *Earl Grey* was a prestige vessel and, in spite of her subsequent achievements, one cannot help feeling that it is a pity that she had such a short life under the Canadian flag.

Earl Grey. MMA MP28.32.8

In the second photo the *Earl Grey* is shown wearing the white ensign. This was probably taken during the 1912 Maritimes tour of the Governor-General, the Duke of Connaught. (She may have been temporarily commissioned into the Naval Service.) In 1914 she again hoisted the white ensign as an RCN ship for the transfer to Russia.

J.D. HAZEN / MIKULA (1) 1916 & 1923-1935

Builder:	Canadian Vickers, Montreal, QC
Date Completed:	1914-15
Tonnage:	3515 (gross)
Dimensions:	275 x 58 x 28 (depth) (ft)
Machinery:	Twin screw steam triple expansion, 568 NHP

The first ship to be built in Canadian Vickers' newly completed shipyard at Montreal. She was named for the Minister of Marine and Fisheries. Although she was laid down in 1914, work was delayed while Vickers concentrated on other war contracts, notably submarines. Russia still needed icebreakers and in 1916 she was, like the *Minto* and *Earl Grey*, sold to the Imperial Russian government and left for Archangel'sk in an uncompleted state (she was commanded by Captain John Read who had taken the

Minto on the same route in 1915). Her Russian name was *Mikula Seleaninovitch*, (a Paul Bunyan-like mythological Russian character who "plowed the steppes" as the ship was intended to plow through the ice). In the confusion of the Bolshevik Revolution that followed, she changed hands from the "whites" to the "reds". In 1918 she was scuttled but was raised by the Allied intervention forces, refitted in England and turned over to the French Navy. In 1919 she was operated by the French in northern Russia. In 1921, the Minister of Marine and Fisheries was informed that an icebreaker was for sale at Cherbourg, and the ship was purchased (from funds allocated for building a new icebreaker) and returned to Canada. She served from 1923 until 1935 as the *Mikula*. She was an effective icebreaker, but a prodigious consumer of coal. She was sold in 1936 and scrapped in Scotland in 1937.

Saurel. DFO

SAUREL 1929-1967

Builder:	Canadian Vickers, Montreal, QC
Date Completed:	1929
Tonnage:	1176 (gross)
Dimensions:	212 x 42 x 14 (ft)
Machinery:	Twin screw steam triple expansion, 3000 IHP
Speed:	14 kts

The *Saurel* belonged to the smaller class of icebreaker used for St. Lawrence River and Gulf service. Her appearance was unmistakable—her profile dominated by a huge single funnel which, as she was a coal burner, often poured out quantities of black smoke. The *Saurel* was retired in 1967 and was scrapped in Italy in 1968.

Saurel. NAC PA207677

N.B. McLEAN 1930-1988

Builder:	Halifax Shipyards, Halifax , NS
Date Completed:	1930
Tonnage:	3254 (gross)
Dimensions:	260 x 60 x 20 (ft)
Machinery:	Twin screw steam triple expansion, 6500 IHP
Speed:	15 kts

This very successful ship was a logical follow-on to the *Montcalm* and *J.D. Hazen* designs. She was named for Nathan B. McLean, a high official of the St. Lawrence ship channel authority, who had led the three-department expedition to Hudson's Bay in 1927 which resulted in the terminus of the railway being changed from Port Nelson to Churchill. Appropriately, the ship was the mainstay of the Hudson Bay route from the 30s to the 70s and the St. Lawrence River and Gulf in the winter. From 1954 to 1970 she also operated in the eastern high Arctic. In the 60s a helicopter deck and hangar were added. In 1970 she made her fortieth and last annual voyage to Hudson Bay and Arctic waters. She continued to be used in the St. Lawrence River and Gulf until she was retired in 1979. Extensive efforts to preserve her as a museum ship and youth training facility at Quebec City were unsuccessful and, after being moved around a succession of lay-up berths, she was finally sold for scrap in 1988. The first photo shows the ship as completed, the second in Coast Guard colours in 1963.

Ernest Lapointe. DFO

Ernest Lapointe. DFO

ERNEST LAPOINTE 1941-1978

Builder:	Davie Shipbuilding Ltd, Montreal, QC
Date Completed:	1941
Tonnage:	1179 (gross)
Dimensions:	172 x 36 x 16 (ft)
Machinery:	Twin screw steam compound, 2000 IHP
Speed:	13 kts

An icebreaker of the smaller class, she was named for a previous Minister of Marine and Fisheries. The ship bringing her triple expansion steam engines from Europe was sunk, so a combination of compound engines intended for tugs was substituted. She thus had two four-cylinder steam engines, each with two high pressure and two low pressure cylinders. During the war she was used to supply the air base at Goose Bay and to assist the *N.B. McLean* in the river. After the loss of the *Lady Grey* in 1955 she was used for ceremonial occasions. In 1958 she made an official visit to Godthaab, Greenland, with a delegation of Canadian Inuit and representatives of the Department of Northern Affairs. In 1964, with a bowsprit added, yards crossed on the foremast and crew in period uniforms, she re-enacted the arrival of the Fathers of Confederation in Charlottetown in the *Queen Victoria*. For most of her service (1941-1967), she was commanded by Captain Robert Marchand. She was retired in 1978 and, since 1980, has been preserved in a gravel-filled dock at the Musée Maritime Bernier at L'Islet sur Mer, Québec.

The first photo shows her in Coast Guard colours and the second shows her impersonating the *Queen Victoria*.

CHAPTER 4

LIGHTHOUSE SUPPLY VESSELS AND BUOY TENDERS

In the mid 1800s, offshore lighthouses were supplied by local craft—often sailing vessels—and the few floating aids that were provided were placed by local authorities and serviced by small craft based in the local area. As traffic increased and more lighthouses were built, the Department of Fisheries and Marine itself began to acquire significant steam vessels. Although classed here as lighthouse supply vessels and buoy tenders, these ships carried out varied duties and would probably have been referred to as "the government steamer." The larger and more powerful ships would do some icebreaking in ports and harbours, just as the icebreakers might carry out lighthouse supply duties in the summer. In the Pacific, the *Quadra* was the symbol of government authority and administration along the remote coasts of British Columbia.

These ships were out in all weathers and, inevitably, there were some losses. The *Simcoe* and *Lambton* foundered. The *Princess Louise, Aberdeen* and *Grenville* were wrecked. The *Montmagny* and *Lady Grey* were lost by collision, as was the *Quadra*, although she was beached and subsequently sold. The *Shamrock* was destroyed by fire. Ships in this category were truly the workhorses of the fleet, as are their successors today.

First Group: Larger vessels over 450 tons

NEWFIELD 1875-1900

Builder:	Thompson, Sunderland, England
Date Completed:	1870
Tonnage:	785 (gross)
Dimensions:	206 x 29 x 17 (depth) (ft)
Machinery:	Single screw steam compound, 90 NHP

An iron vessel built for the coastal coal trade. Purchased in 1875 for service as a lighthouse supply vessel and buoy tender in Nova Scotia. The woodcut, published in the *Canadian Illustrated News* for December 1877, shows her leaving for France with the Canadian exhibits for the Paris Exposition of 1878. She is rigged as a brigantine and has the typical rudimentary turtle-backed deckhouse of the 1870s. We can be sure that in later life the rig was reduced and a derrick fitted. The *Newfield* was wrecked at White Cove, Digby Neck, Nova Scotia in 1900.

PRINCESS LOUISE 1882
LANSDOWNE 1883-1917

Builder:	O'Brien at Maccan, NS
Date Completed:	1882 and 1883
Tonnage:	680 (gross)
Dimensions:	189 x 32 x 13.5 (ft)
Machinery:	Single screw steam compound, 80 NHP

The *Princess Louise* was a wooden lighthouse supply vessel and buoy tender named for Queen Victoria's fourth daughter, who was the consort of the Governor-General, the Marquess of Lorne. On completion, without machinery, she was taken in tow by the *Newfield* for the passage to Halifax but the towing cable parted in a sudden gale and the *Princess Louise* was driven ashore on Point Prim, with the loss of her Captain and seven of the crew. An order for a similar vessel was immediately placed with the same builder. The *Lansdowne,* named for the new Governor-General, was successfully completed and received the machinery intended for the *Princess Louise.* She served on the East Coast until 1917 when she was retired. Registry closed in 1920.

QUADRA (1) 1892-1917

Builder:	Fleming and Ferguson, Paisley, Scotland
Date Completed:	1892
Tonnage:	573 (gross)
Dimensions:	174 x 31 x 13.5 (depth) (ft)
Machinery:	Single screw steam quadruple expansion, 120 NHP
Speed:	11.5 kts

A steel lighthouse tender and buoy vessel to replace the *Sir James Douglas* in British Columbia waters. In the 1890s, the *Quadra* was the principal government vessel on the BC coast.

Her Commander, Captain John T. Walbran, was a magistrate and the ship's crew included a police officer. The *Quadra's* government career came to an end in February 1917 when she was damaged in a collision with the Canadian Pacific Railway vessel *Charmer* and was beached to prevent her foundering. The wreck was sold and, after salvage, was converted to an ore carrier. By 1925 the former law-enforcement vessel had become a rum-runner. She was seized by the United States Coast Guard, taken to San Francisco and sold for scrap.

Aberdeen. NAC PA206964

ABERDEEN 1894-1923

Builder:	Fleming and Ferguson, Paisley, Scotland
Date Completed:	1894
Tonnage:	674 (gross)
Dimensions:	180 x 31 x 19 (depth) (ft)
Machinery:	Single screw steam quadruple expansion
Speed:	13 kts

A steel lighthouse supply and buoy vessel named for the Governor-General, the Earl of Aberdeen. In the early photo of the ship running speed trials, she is flush decked and is able to set fore and aft sail. The later photo shows that a high foc's'le was added—no doubt to cope with Canadian East Coast conditions—and a heavy derrick has replaced the standing gaffs. She commenced her service on the Atlantic but was later transferred to the Quebec agency, then back to Saint John NB in 1904.

Aberdeen. DFO

On 13 October 1923, the *Aberdeen* stranded on Seal Island, NS and became a total loss.

Druid. DFO

Druid. DFO

DRUID (2) 1902-1946

Builder:	Fleming and Ferguson, Paisley, Scotland
Date Completed:	1902
Tonnage:	503 (gross)
Dimensions:	160 x 30 x 13 (depth) (ft)
Machinery:	Twin screw steam triple expansion, 800 IHP
Speed:	10 kts

A steel lighthouse supply and buoy vessel. The first of the single-well-decked, twin screw, buoy tenders of a general design that is still the norm for this type of vessel. The *Druid* was a sturdy, long-lasting ship. The top photo shows her in her early days; the other was taken in 1944. She was sold in 1946, converted to motor and continued in commercial service under various names until she was scuttled in December, 1986.

LADY LAURIER 1902-1959

Builder:	Fleming and Ferguson, Paisley, Scotland
Date Completed:	1902
Tonnage:	1051 (gross)
Dimensions:	210 x 34 x 18 (depth) (ft)
Machinery:	Twin screw steam triple expansion, 1800 IHP
Speed:	13 kts

Another Fleming and Ferguson product, named for the wife of the Prime Minister, Sir Wilfried Laurier. She was intended to be a cable ship as well as a lighthouse and buoy tender. The cable tank was soon removed along with the sheaves but she retained the characteristic cable ship bow profile to the end. The *Lady Laurier* serviced the lights and aids along the Nova Scotia coast and on occasion as far as Cape Race, Newfoundland. She was the principal supply vessel for Sable Island. She assisted many ships in distress—notably, in 1911, when she helped to free HMCS *Niobe* (Canada's first cruiser) which had grounded on Southwest Ledge off Cape Sable. After a long and useful life the *Lady Laurier* was retired in 1959 and sold for breaking up in 1960.

PRINCESS 1906-1920

Built:	Grangemouth, Scotland
Date Completed:	1896
Tonnage:	542 (gross)
Dimensions:	165 x 26 x 17.1 (depth) (ft)
Machinery:	Single screw steam triple expansion, 90 NHP

A coastal passenger and cargo steamer purchased from the Charlottetown Steam Navigation Company in 1906 and converted to a lighthouse supply vessel and buoy tender in the Atlantic. Sold to Peruvian owners in 1920.

MONTMAGNY (1) 1909-1914

Built: Canadian Government Shipyard, Sorel, QC
Date Completed: 1909
Tonnage: 1269 (gross)
Dimensions: 213 x 35 x19.5 (depth) (ft)
Machinery: Single screw triple expansion, 148 NHP

A steel lighthouse supply vessel and buoy tender. In April 1912 she was one of two ships—the other was the cable ship *Mackay Bennett*—sent to the scene of the sinking of the *Titanic* with the melancholy duty of recovering bodies. She was occasionally employed as a light vessel and was known then as Lightship No. 21. The *Montmagny* herself met a tragic end. On 18 September 1914, while en route to supply lighthouses on the north shore of the Gulf, with lightkeepers and their families on board, she was rammed and sunk by the collier *Lingan*. The ship sank in four minutes and fourteen people, eleven of whom were children, lost their lives. The accident occurred within sight of the town for which she was named.

SIMCOE (1) 1909-1917

Builder:	Swan Hunter, Wallsend-on-Tyne, England
Date Completed:	1909
Tonnage:	913 (gross)
Dimensions:	180 x 35 x 15 (depth) (ft)
Machinery:	Twin screw steam triple expansion, 217 NHP

A steel lighthouse supply vessel and buoy tender. The *Simcoe* and the smaller *Lambton* were the first Marine and Fisheries ships for permanent service in the Great Lakes. Both met tragic ends. In 1917 the *Simcoe* was en route to Saint John NB to relieve the *Dollard*. She worked her way there and had just deliv-

ered supplies from Sydney to the isolated Bird Island lighthouse when she was caught in a severe storm. The radio operator at Grindstone radio station received a hurried distress signal and that was the last that was heard of her and the 44 people on board. No other ships were in the vicinity, southwest of the Magdalen Islands. The sturdy twin screw buoy tenders of the *Simcoe's* type were expected to be able to survive the worst storms. One possible reason for her loss: if large buoys on deck or in the hold had broken loose they could have caused enough damage to flood the hold.

Estevan. DFO

ESTEVAN 1912-1969

Builder:	Collingwood Shipbuilding, ON
Date Completed:	1912
Tonnage:	1161 (gross)
Dimensions:	212 x 38 x 12 (ft)
Machinery:	Twin screw steam triple expansion, 1500 IHP
Speed:	12.5 kts

A steel lighthouse supply vessel and buoy tender. The *Estevan* was similar in design to the other twin screw buoy tenders, *Simcoe* and *Dollard,* all developed from the design of the *Druid.* On completion, she proceeded to the Pacific Coast via the Straits of Magellan, arriving there to commence work in 1913. In 1935 she was re-boiled and in 1958 converted from coal to oil firing. At the time of her retirement in 1969, the *Estevan* had the dis-

Estevan. DFO

tinction of being the longest serving ship (57 years) in the Canadian Marine Service and the Canadian Coast Guard which succeeded it. She was towed to Japan for scrapping in 1970.

Dollard. NAC PA207016

Aranmore. NAC PA206883

Grenville. DFO

DOLLARD 1913-1961

Builder:	Kingston Shipbuilding, Kingston, ON
Date Completed:	1913
Tonnage:	835 (gross)
Dimensions:	170 x 31.5 x 15.5 (depth) (ft)
Machinery:	Twin screw steam triple expansion, 1000 IHP
Speed:	11 kts

A steel lighthouse supply vessel and buoy tender. Probably, considering her name, intended for the Quebec agency but was stationed at Saint John, NB. She was considered under-powered for the Bay of Fundy conditions and was to have been relieved by the *Simcoe* in 1917, but when that ship sank off the Magdalen Islands, she soldiered on until she was sold in 1961. Converted to a freighter, she was abandoned in the Caribbean in 1968.

ARANMORE 1914-1939

Builder:	W.B.Thompson, Dundee, Scotland
Date Completed:	1890
Tonnage:	1170 (gross)
Dimensions:	241.5 x 35 x 16 (depth) (ft)
Machinery:	Single screw steam triple expansion, 1500 IHP
Speed:	13 kts

An iron coastal freighter purchased in 1914. The *Aranmore* was employed as a lighthouse supply vessel and buoy tender in the Atlantic. She was sold (commercial) in 1939 and eventually sank off Haiti in 1946 when under Cuban ownership.

GRENVILLE (2) 1915-1968

Builder:	Polson Iron Works, Toronto
Date Completed:	1915
Tonnage:	497 (gross)
Dimensions:	164 x 30 x 9.5 (ft)
Machinery:	Single screw steam triple expansion, 900 IHP
Speed:	11.5 kts

A steel lighthouse supply vessel and buoy tender that served faithfully for over fifty years. In December 1968 she was wrecked when driven by an ice sheet against the St. Louis bridge in Lake St. Francis. The crew managed to climb onto the abutments of the bridge and were saved.

SAFEGUARDER 1929-1967

Builder:	Day, Summers and Co, Southampton, England
Date Completed:	1914
Tonnage:	665 (gross)
Dimensions:	160 x 29 x 12 (ft)
Machinery:	Twin screw steam triple expansion, 1350 IHP
Speed:	13.5 kts

A steel lighthouse supply vessel and buoy tender, originally named *Safeguard*, purchased in 1929 for service on the Great Lakes. Sold 1967.

St Heliers. DFO

ST. HELIERS 1930-1960

Builder:	Ferguson Bros., Port Glasgow, Scotland
Date Completed:	1919
Tonnage:	930 (gross)
Dimensions:	190 x 29 x 16 (depth) (ft)
Machinery:	Single screw steam triple expansion, 1200 IHP
Speed:	11.5 kts

Originally a British Saint class naval tug like the *St. Finbarr*, which became the *Franklin (1)*. Purchased 1930 and lengthened. The reconstruction resulted in a normal buoy tender configuration. The *St. Heliers* was employed as a lighthouse supply and buoy vessel on the Great Lakes. She was sold (commercial) 1960.

Alberni. DFO

ALBERNI 1936-1961

Built:	Government Shipyard, Sorel, QC
Date Completed:	1927
Tonnage:	502 (gross)
Dimensions:	157.3 x 30.7 x 12.3 (ft)
Machinery:	Twin screw compound, 360 IHP
Speed:	8 kts

A former coal barge (No. 7). Converted to a lighthouse supply vessel and buoy tender in 1936. From 1937 to 1960 the *Alberni* was stationed at Prince Rupert, BC. She was retired in 1960 and sold in 1961.

Franklin. NAC PA207017

FRANKLIN (1) 1939-1958

Builder:	Fleming and Ferguson, Paisley, Scotland
Date Completed:	1919
Tonnage:	613 (gross)
Dimensions:	136 x 29 x 13.5 (depth) (ft)
Machinery:	Single screw steam triple expansion, 1200 IHP
Speed:	11.5 kts

A wartime Saint class naval tug, originally named *St. Finbar*, purchased for the Department of the Interior in 1923. Transferred to the Department of Transport in 1939. The foc'sle was extended for the length of the vessel which effectively hid her tug origins. Used as a lighthouse supply and buoy vessel on the Great Lakes and also as a lightship. Sold 1958. Broken up 1961.

Chesterfield. DFO

CHESTERFIELD 1943-1967

Builder:	Collingwood Shipbuilding, ON
Date Completed:	1928
Tonnage:	734 (gross)
Dimensions:	180 x 32 x 12 (ft)
Machinery:	Single screw steam triple expansion, 700 IHP

Originally a steel self-propelled hopper-dredger, she was converted in 1943 to a lighthouse supply vessel and buoy tender for the Quebec agency. Retired 1967 and sold (commercial) 1969.

Second Group: Small buoy tenders under 450 tons

GLENDON 1874-1881

Built:	Saint John, NB
Date Completed:	1872
Tonnage:	266 (gross)
Dimensions:	128 x 30 x 9 (depth) (ft)
Machinery:	Single screw steam single cylinder, 21 NHP

A wooden three-masted schooner with an auxiliary engine, purchased in 1874. She was also sometimes used for fisheries patrol. Laid up 1881 and sold 1885.

SHAMROCK 1898-1928

Builder:	J.C. Kaine, QC
Date Completed:	1898
Tonnage:	237 (gross)
Dimensions:	117 x 25 x 10 (depth) (ft)
Machinery:	Single screw steam compound, 61 NHP

A small wooden buoy tender. Destroyed by fire at Sorel, Quebec, in 1928.

BRANT (1) 1899-1928

Builder:	John White, Charlottetown, PEI
Date Completed:	1899
Tonnage:	141 (gross)
Dimensions:	100 x 19 x 8 (depth) (ft)
Machinery:	Single screw steam compound, 33 NHP

A small wooden lighthouse supply vessel and buoy tender. Sold (commercial) 1928.

Shamrock. NAC PA207018

Brant. PEIPA 3466/HF77.234

Scout. DFO

SCOUT 1902-1934

Builder:	J.R. Miller, Cardinal, ON
Date Completed:	1900
Tonnage:	176 (gross)
Dimensions:	104 x 26 x 9 (depth) (ft)
Machinery:	Single screw steam compound, 27 NHP

A wooden vessel built for the Department of Railways and Canals and transferred to Marine and Fisheries in 1902. Employed as a gas buoy tender between Montreal and Kingston. In 1906, the Captain and three of her crew were killed when a gas buoy exploded. The ship was repaired and lasted until 1934. The photo shows her after alterations.

ROUVILLE 1906-1931

Built:	Canadian Government Shipyard, QC
Date Completed:	1906
Tonnage:	301 (gross)
Dimensions:	130 x 26 x 12.5 (ft)
Machinery:	Single screw steam compound, 54 NHP

A wooden vessel intended for use on Hudson Bay by the RCMP, but taken over and used as a buoy tender in the St. Lawrence ship channel. Sunk in 1931.

NEWINGTON 1908-1937

Builder:	Cook, Welton and Gemmell, Hull, England
Date Completed:	1899
Tonnage:	193 (gross)
Dimensions:	115 x 21 x 11.5 (depth) (ft)
Machinery:	Single screw steam triple expansion, 58 NHP

An iron trawler, purchased in 1908 and converted to a lighthouse supply and buoy tender for the BC agency. Taken up by the Navy in 1914 and fitted to lay mines, then used as a patrol vessel. Returned 1920. Sold (commercial) 1937. Sunk 1959.

LEEBRO

Chartered 1909-1912

Builder:	W. Turpel, Victoria, BC
Date Completed:	1908
Tonnage:	323 (gross)
Dimensions:	124 x 29 x 11 (depth) (ft)
Machinery:	Single screw steam compound, 22 NHP

A wooden vessel chartered by the Marine and Fisheries Victoria, BC agency from 1909 to 1912 for lighthouse supply and general duties. In 1967 she was converted to represent the original Hudson Bay Company paddle steamer *Beaver*. Broken up 1977.

Newington. VMM

Leebro. VMM 12487 ; 1543

Lambton. DFO

LAMBTON 1909-1922

Built:	Canadian Government Shipyard, QC
Date Completed:	1909
Tonnage:	323 (gross)
Dimensions:	108 x 25 x 13 (depth) (ft)
Machinery:	Single screw steam triple expansion, 90 NHP

A steel lighthouse supply vessel and buoy tender, stationed at the Parry Sound agency. In April 1922, on the first run of the season with ice still on Lake Superior and in very bad weather, she was lost with all hands: a total of 22 crew and lightkeepers. She was last seen by another ship near Caribou Island, about 75 miles northeast of Sault Ste. Marie, apparently with steering problems but not in distress. The details of the *Lambton's* last hours were never established.

Argenteuil. DFO

ARGENTEUIL 1917-1960

Built:	Canadian Government Shipyard, Sorel, QC
Date Completed:	1917
Tonnage:	165 (gross)
Dimensions:	100 x 21 x 5.5 (ft)
Machinery:	Single screw steam compound, 16 NHP

A composite buoy tender for the Ottawa River. Sold (commercial) in 1960. Sunk in 1962 near Lauzon, Quebec.

Concretia. NAC PA136349

CONCRETIA 1918-1935

Built:	Montreal, QC
Date Completed:	1918
Tonnage:	320 (gross)
Dimensions:	126 x 22 x 10 (depth) (ft)
Machinery:	Single screw steam compound, 24 NHP

An experimental wartime vessel built of ferro-cement (others were built in the Second World War). Completed as a lighthouse supply and buoy vessel, she was sold in 1935 and existed as a stripped hulk in Kingston harbour, where she was used for a time as a mooring wharf. In 1979 she was refloated and converted to a sailing yacht (!) departing for the Caribbean in 1982.

Laurentian. DFO

LAURENTIAN 1919-1946

Builder:	Cook, Welton and Gemmell, Hull, England
Date Completed:	1902
Tonnage:	355 (gross)
Dimensions:	149 x 24 x 11 (ft)
Machinery:	Single screw steam triple expansion, 84 NHP

A steel trawler (ex *King Edward*) acquired by Davie of Lévis, Quebec, in 1911. Renamed *Laurentian* and chartered to the Customs Preventive Service 1911-13. Sold to the RCN in 1917 and used as a patrol vessel until 1919, when she was transferred to Marine and Fisheries as a lighthouse supply vessel and buoy tender. Retired 1946. Scrapped 1947.

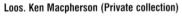

Loos. Ken Macpherson (Private collection)

LOOS 1922-1937

Builder:	Canadian Vickers, Montreal, QC
Date Completed:	1918
Tonnage:	357 (gross)
Dimensions:	130 x 25 x 13 (depth) (ft)
Machinery:	Single screw steam triple expansion, 480 IHP
Speed:	10 kts

A naval trawler of standard wartime design. Taken over and completed as a lighthouse supply and buoy vessel in 1922. Sold (commercial) 1937 but again taken up by the Navy in 1940 and used as a gate vessel. Returned to owners 1946 and broken up in 1949. Sister ships *St. Eloi, St. Julien, Messines & Vimy* were converted to lightships. *Arras, Arleux & Givenchy* became fisheries patrol vessels. (See Chapter 6).

Brant. NAC PA149546

BRANT (2) 1928-1966

Built:	Canadian Government Shipyard, QC
Date Completed:	1928
Tonnage:	285 (gross)
Dimensions:	125 x 23 x 12 (depth) (ft)
Machinery:	Single screw steam triple expansion, 350 IHP
Speed:	10 kts

A steel trawler-type lighthouse supply vessel and buoy tender. Stationed at the Dartmouth agency. Retired 1966 and sold 1967.

Bernier. NAC PA206971

BERNIER 1930-1960

Builder:	Davie Shipbuilding Ltd, Lauzon, QC
Date Completed:	1918
Tonnage:	317 (gross)
Dimensions:	123 x 23 x 14 (depth) (ft)
Machinery:	Single screw steam triple expansion, 500 IHP
Speed:	9.5 kts

A wartime naval trawler, ex *Mardep,* ex *Labrador,* ex TR45. Purchased 1930 and converted to a lighthouse supply vessel for the Dartmouth agency. Sold (commercial) 1960.

CHAPTER 5

CUSTOMS PREVENTIVE SERVICE AND RCMP PATROL VESSELS

Between 1897 and 1931 the Customs Preventive Service of the Department of Customs and Excise operated a fleet of lightly armed patrol cruisers whose business was to detect and prevent the smuggling of goods, chiefly liquor, into Canada. The larger of these vessels were stationed on the East Coast and the Gulf of St. Lawrence, with smaller craft on the Great Lakes and in the Pacific. The *Constance*, a Marine and Fisheries vessel was transferred to the Preventive Service. Other ships were purchased and quite a large number were chartered for periods varying from a few weeks to two or three years. Some of these belonged to other government departments and came with their own crews. It was not until 1914 that the first purpose-built Customs cruiser, the *Margaret*, joined the fleet, but was immediately requisitioned by the RCN for service during the First World War.

In the 1920s, preventive patrols continued, not always to the pleasure of local law-makers. In 1921 a cruiser intercepted the ship carrying the "election booze" and the charter of that particular vessel was immediately terminated. On another occasion a vessel arrested just inside the three nautical mile limit was released and the cargo returned as the magistrate chose to interpret the limit as three statute miles. In this period rum running became so prevalent that in 1927-1931 the fleet had to be expanded. Fast vessels which looked like miniature warships were constructed, several motor yachts were purchased and seized vessels were also incorporated into the service.

In 1932 the provincial police forces of the three maritime provinces were absorbed into the RCMP. At the same time the RCMP took over the vessels of the Customs Preventive Service of what was now the Department of National Revenue. Six aircraft of the RCAF were also assigned to RCMP Marine Operations and an effective anti-smuggling organization was established. The Marine Branch had the benefit of four modern vessels just completed and went on to build three more. The larger ships were based at the naval dockyard in Halifax and relied on the Navy for maintenance and training, while crews wore naval type uniforms. Thus, on the outbreak of war in 1939, it was not difficult to incorporate the majority of the vessels and their crews into the Royal Canadian Navy, while some of the smaller craft and their crews became part of the Royal Canadian Air Force and were used for air-sea rescue purposes.

CONSTANCE 1892-1908

Builder:	Polson Iron Works, Owen Sound, ON
Date Completed:	1892
Tonnage:	185 (gross)
Dimensions:	116 x 20 x 11 (ft)
Machinery:	Single screw steam compound, 50 NHP
Speed:	11 kts
Armament:	3 machine guns

Built for Marine and Fisheries in 1892 but transferred to the Department of Customs on completion. In 1897 she was under the control of the Customs Preventive Service, based at Gaspé. Returned to Marine and Fisheries in 1908. Naval service 1914-19. Sold (commercial) 1920 and used as a coastal steamer in the 20s and early 30s, but chartered by Customs Preventive Service 1928-29.

CHRISTINE 1908-1911

Built:	Glasgow, Scotland
Date Completed:	1881
Tonnage:	140 (gross)
Dimensions:	126 x 17.2 x 9.2 (ft)
Machinery:	Single screw steam compound, 40 NHP
Speed:	10 kts
Armament:	small arms

An iron vessel purchased by Marine and Fisheries and transferred to the Customs Preventive Service to replace the *Constance*. Sold 1911 and used as a ferry between Quebec and Ile d'Orleans. Sunk 1915 after collision with submarine H1.

MARGARET 1914-1932

Builder:	Woolton Works, Southampton, England
Date Completed:	1914
Tonnage:	756 (gross)
Dimensions:	182.4 x 32.3 x 15 (ft)
Machinery:	Twin screw steam triple expansion, 2000 IHP
Speed:	15.5 kts
Armament:	Two 6 pdr QF

The first ship built specifically for the Customs Preventive Service, the *Margaret* was turned over to the Navy soon after completion and served as a naval patrol vessel throughout the First World War. Returned to the Customs Preventive Service in 1919 and continued on customs patrols, usually based at Gaspé, until 1931. She had been converted from coal to oil burning in 1925. Transferred to the RCMP in 1932 but not active. Sold to some Brazilian dissidents but captured by the Brazilian Navy in 1935 and converted to a hydrographic vessel, the *Rio Branco*.

Margaret. MMA MP37.6.3

GRIB 1920-1926

Built:	Sandefjord, Norway
Date Completed:	1907
Tonnage:	140 (gross)
Dimensions:	94.5 x 18.7 x 10.2 (ft)
Machinery:	Single screw steam compound, 43 NHP
Speed:	10 kts
Armament:	small arms

A former Norwegian whaler, registered at Montreal in 1915. Wrecked 1917 but salvaged. Transferred from the Naval Service 1920. Customs Preventive service 1920-26. Sold 1928 and used as a tug at Halifax.

PATROL BOAT No.IV 1924-1934
BAR OFF 1927-1936

Built:	New York, NY
Date Completed:	1917 and 1918
Tonnage:	76 (gross)
Dimensions:	87.8 x 14.6 x 8 (ft)
Machinery:	As built: triple screw gasoline engines, 660 BHP
Speed:	18 kts
Re-engined in 1928:	*No.IV* with two 180 BHP diesels; *Bar Off* with three 80 BHP diesels. Speed after being re-engined:15 kts
Armament:	One 3 pdr QF

Seized rum-runners, both former American submarine chasers. *Patrol Boat No. IV* , ex *Stumble Inn*, was seized in Lake Erie in 1924. She was based at North Sydney. The *Bar Off*, also written *Baroff* was *Bo-Peep* as a smuggler. She was based at Gaspé. Both transferred to the RCMP in 1932. Fate of *Patrol Boat No. IV* not known. *Bar Off* was disposed of by the War Assets Corporation in 1945.

CUSTOMS PREVENTIVE SERVICE AND RCMP PATROL VESSELS

Scatari. NAC PA209431

SCATARI 1928-1939

Built:	Orillia, ON
Date Completed:	1926
Tonnage:	41 (gross)
Dimensions:	71.7 x 13.7 x 6 (ft)
Machinery:	one diesel and two gasoline engines
Speed:	35 kts
Armament:	small arms

Originally the fast rum runner *174*, used to transfer contraband from the well known schooner *I'm Alone* from outside of territorial limits, to the US mainland. She was seized by the *Bar Off* at Chaleur in 1928 and based at Cheticamp, NS. Transferred to the RCMP in 1932 and to the Navy in 1939. Speed probably exaggerated.

Conestoga. MMA MP28.91.1

CONESTOGA 1927-1932

Built:	Racine, WI
Date Completed:	1896
Tonnage:	168 (gross)
Dimensions:	136 x 18.3 x 10.3 (ft)
Machinery:	Single screw steam, 51 NHP
Speed:	14 kts
Armament:	small arms

Formerly the yacht *Pathfinder*, of distinctively military appearance. Chartered in 1927 and purchased in 1928. Laid up 1932 and returned to original owner in 1933.

BAYHOUND 1928-1936

Built:	New York, NY
Date Completed:	1910
Tonnage:	135 (gross)
Dimensions:	114 x 17.2 x 6 (ft)
Machinery:	Single screw diesel, 400 BHP
Armament:	small arms

Formerly the yacht *Tillicum*, acquired 1928. In 1932 she was based at Yarmouth, NS. Transferred to the RCMP in 1932. Out of service 1936.

Fleur de Lis. RCMP Museum, Regina

FLEUR DE LIS
1929-1939
PREVENTOR
1929-1937

Builder:	Canadian Vickers, Montreal, QC
Date Completed:	1929
Tonnage:	316 (gross)
Dimensions:	164.8 x 21.1 x 11.7 (ft)
Machinery:	Triple screw diesel, 1800 BH
Speed:	18 kts
Armament:	One 6 pdr QF

Fast vessels on miniature warship lines, built for the Customs Preventive Service and transferred to the RCMP in 1932. *Preventor* was sold in 1937. *Fleur de Lis* was transferred to the RCN in 1939 and served as a patrol craft at Halifax. She was sold in 1945 and removed from the register in 1953.

Preventor. RCMP Museum, Regina

ALACHASSE

1931-1939

Built: Sorel, QC

ADVERSUS

1931-1939

Built:	Orillia, ON
Date Completed:	1931
Tonnage:	157 (gross)
Dimensions:	116.4 x 19 x 11.3 (ft)
Machinery:	Twin screw diesel, 750 BHP
Speed:	12 kts
Armament:	One machine gun

Built for the Preventive Service and transferred to the RCMP after completion. *Alachasse* was based at Shediac NB. *Adversus* was first based at North Sydney, NS, but was transferred to the Pacific in 1933. She returned to the East Coast in 1939 when both vessels were taken over by the RCN. *Adversus* was wrecked in December 1941 and *Alachasse* was sold in 1945.

Adversus. NAC PA209445

Alachasse. NAC PA207021

ULNA 1931-1939

Built:	Southampton, England
Date Completed:	1909
Tonnage:	167 (gross)
Dimensions:	115.7 x 18.5 x 10.2 (ft)
Machinery:	Single screw steam triple expansion, 41 NHP
Armament:	One 3 pdr QF

A former yacht, chartered in 1931 and purchased by the RCMP in 1932. Based at Gaspé. Returned to owner in 1939 for use as a coastal freighter.

Ulna. NAC PA209432

Chartered Patrol Vessels
(Major vessels chartered by the Customs Preventive Service in the period 1897-1931)

1897:	*Victoria* (Schooner)
1897:	*Gladiator* (Tug)
1898:	*Stanley* (Marine and Fisheries icebreaker)
1909-10:	*Gladiator* (Tug)
1911-13:	*Laurentian* (Later a naval auxiliary and eventually a buoy tender)
1916:	*Dollard* (Marine and Fisheries lighthouse supply vessel)
1917:	*Restless* (Steam yacht)
1917:	*Canso* (Department of Public Works tug)
1918:	*Lisgar* (Department of Public Works tug)
1921-22:	*Restless* (Steam yacht)
1922-24:	*Sagamore* (Steam yacht)
1926-27:	*Mayita* (Steam yacht)
1926-27:	*Cartier* (Hydrographic survey vessel)
1927:	*Hochelaga* (Former yacht, naval auxiliary and ferry)
1927:	*Lady Laurier* (Marine and Fisheries lighthouse supply vessel)
1927-28:	*Bayfield (2)* (Hydrographic survey vessel)
1927-28:	*Vigilant* (Former fisheries patrol vessel)
1928-29:	*Constance* (Former customs and fisheries patrol vessel, see above)

Vessels built for the RCMP Marine Section

LAURIER 1936-1939
MACDONALD 1936-1939

Builder:	Morton Engineering & Drydock Ltd, Quebec City, QC
Date Completed:	1936
Tonnage:	201 (gross)
Dimensions:	113 x 21 x 10.3 (ft)
Machinery:	Twin screw diesel
Speed:	12 kts

The first major patrol craft designed and built for the RCMP. Both ships served in the RCN from 1939 to 1945. In 1946 they were both turned over to the Fisheries Department for service on the Pacific coast (see Chapter 18). *Macdonald* was renamed *Howay* but *Laurier* retained her original name.

Laurier. NAC PA209439

Macdonald. MMA

FRENCH (1) 1938-1939

Built:	Lauzon, QC
Date Completed:	1938
Tonnage:	226 (gross)
Dimensions:	138 x 22 x 10.7 (ft)
Machinery:	Twin screw diesel
Speed:	12 kts

The *French* was taken up by the RCN at the outbreak of war in 1939 and served as a patrol boat. Sold (commercial) in 1946.

CHAPTER 6

FISHERIES PATROL VESSELS

After the 1812-14 war with the United States, the colonial authorities soon found that the Royal Navy, whose job it was to enforce fisheries regulations, had little enthusiasm or expertise for the task, nor were its ships suitable. They therefore provided fisheries patrol vessels of their own, usually schooners. Some were chartered on a regular basis but those built for the government included the Nova Scotia schooner *Daring* (1851) and the later *Kingfisher.* The first *Vigilant* was an American schooner seized in 1886 for fishing illegally. These vessels looked just like other fishing craft and so could approach unrecognized. They were lightly armed with a 9 pdr cannon and the crew were issued with small arms. A particularly well known and effective schooner was *La Canadienne* which operated in the Gulf of St. Lawrence under the direction of the magistrate (later a senator) Dr. Pierre Fortin, who was known as "Le Roi du Golfe." In *Usque ad Mare*, Thomas Appleton has described the work of this remarkable man.

In the latter part of the century, fisheries cruisers continued to be lightly armed with small quick-firing guns and carried small arms for use by boarding parties. To emphasize the semi-military nature of their duties, officers of the Marine and Fisheries Department were issued with swords as part of their dress uniform. Typically, the patrol during the main fishing season comprised both government and chartered vessels. In 1888, on the East Coast and Gulf of St. Lawrence, it consisted of *Acadia*, *La Canadienne* and *Vigilant* (schooner), with two chartered steamers (one for use on Lake Erie) and four chartered schooners. On the West Coast the *Sir James Douglas* added fisheries patrol to all her other duties.

In the 1890s and early 1900s, the fisheries cruisers took on a decidedly martial air and looked like small warships, although only the *Canada* could be considered as an effective naval vessel. After the First World War, there was a return to the use of ships that looked like their quarry, as war-built naval trawlers replaced the old patrol craft.

The Department of Fisheries was briefly independent from 1884 to 1892. In 1914 responsibility for fisheries and customs patrols was transferred to the Royal Canadian Navy, along with the patrol craft. Some ships continued their regular duties but others were commissioned during the First World War and flew the white ensign. In 1920 the ships and personnel were returned to Marine and Fisheries or the Department of Revenue, as appropriate.

In 1927 Marine and Fisheries became separate branches, and in 1930, separate departments. (Further administrative changes are described in Part 2)

LA CANADIENNE

LA CANADIENNE (1)

1855-1874

Builder:	Lee, QC
Date Completed:	1855
Tonnage:	101 (gross)
Dimensions:	92 x 23 x 10 (depth) (ft)

A very fast schooner and an effective fisheries protection vessel. She was built to the order of Dr. Pierre Fortin when the old paddle steamer *Doris* proved unsatisfactory. In later years she was used for lighthouse supply and while so employed was wrecked on St. Paul's Island in 1874. Other schooners, some chartered, were also used for fisheries patrols.

The drawing by F.R. Berchem is based on a contemporary woodcut.

La Canadienne. Ron Beaupré (Private Collection)

LA CANADIENNE (2)

1881-1906

Builder:	Robert Duncan at Port Glasgow, Scotland
Date Completed:	1880
Tonnage:	372 (gross)
Dimensions:	154 x 23 x 11 (depth) (ft)
Machinery:	Single screw steam compound, 60 NHP (she appears to have received a triple expansion engine later).

An iron vessel built as the *Foxhound*, purchased in 1881. She was used as a fisheries patrol vessel and for general duties. In 1906, she was transferred to the hydrographic service (see Chapter 7). In the crowded harbour scene she is the vessel at the right.

Acadia. DFO

ACADIA (1) 1885-1910

Builder:	J. Roach & Son, Chester, PA
Date Completed:	1880
Tonnage:	520 (gross)
Dimensions:	182.5 x 23.5 x 19 (depth) (ft)
Machinery:	Single screw steam compound, 155 NHP

An iron vessel built as the *Yosemite*. Purchased 1885. An early photo shows her with a small cannon mounted forward. Scrapped in 1910.

PELICAN 1889-1898

Builder:	Devonport Royal Navy Dockyard, England
Date Completed:	1877
Tonnage:	638 (gross)
Dimensions:	170 x 36 x 15.5 (ft)
Machinery:	Single screw horizontal compound, 1050 IHP
Speed:	12 kts

A composite former Royal Navy sloop employed as a fisheries patrol vessel from 1889. In 1891 she rescued the Dominion Coal Co vessel *Cape Breton* which had run aground at Cape Race on her maiden voyage. Laid up 1898. Purchased by the Hudson Bay Company in 1902 and made 20 annual trips north. Sold by them in 1920 and in 1923, while under tow, she ran aground on Sable Island. Rescued by *Ocean Eagle* (Chapter 8) and brought to Sydney NS where she was laid up and eventually sank. Raised, towed to sea and scuttled in August 1950.

Curlew. DFO

CONSTANCE 1892-1920
CURLEW 1892-1921
PETREL 1892-1923

Builder:	Polson Iron Works, Owen Sound, ON
Date Completed:	1892
Tonnage:	185 (gross)
Dimensions:	116 x 20 x 11 (ft) (*Petrel* 192 (gross), beam 22 ft)
Machinery:	Single screw steam compound, 50 NHP
Speed:	11 kts
Armament:	3 machine guns

Fisheries cruisers with ram bows, resembling some contemporary gunboats. *Constance* was assigned to the Customs Preventive Service, *Curlew* was used for fisheries patrol on the East Coast and *Petrel* was stationed in the Great Lakes until 1904, then joined *Curlew* on fisheries protection duties in the Atlantic. *Constance* returned to fisheries patrol in 1908. In 1912 they were

Petrel. Ron Beaupré (Private Collection)

all fitted for minesweeping and in 1914 they were taken over by the RCN and used as patrol or examination vessels in between performing their regular duties. Armed with three machine guns. All sold after the First World War.

Gulnare. NAC PA207090

GULNARE (4) 1902-1925

Builder:	C. Connel, Glasgow
Date Completed:	1893
Tonnage:	262 (gross)
Dimensions:	137 x 20 x 13.5 (depth) (ft)
Machinery:	Single screw steam triple expansion, 64 NHP

A steel trawler type vessel purchased in 1902 for fisheries protection duties. Placed under naval control in 1914, she was used in 1918 and 1919 for contraband patrols. The *Gulnare* was returned to Marine and Fisheries in 1920 and employed principally for tidal surveys. Rebuilt as a lightship in 1925. Broken up in 1946.

Kestrel. VMM 14232 ; 1442

KESTREL 1903-1912

Builder:	A. Wallace, Vancouver, BC
Date Completed:	1903
Tonnage:	311 (gross)
Dimensions:	126.5 x 24 x 12 (depth) (ft)
Machinery:	Single screw steam compound, 59 NHP

A wooden vessel used on fisheries protection duties on the Pacific Coast. Sold 1912. The photo shows that her design was influenced by that of the *Curlew* class.

VIGILANT (2) 1904-1924

Builder:	Polson Iron Works, Toronto, ON
Date Completed:	1904
Tonnage:	396 (gross)
Dimensions:	175 x 22 x 10 (ft)
Machinery:	Twin screw steam triple expansion, 130 NHP, 1250 IHP
Speed:	17 kts
Armament:	One or two 3 pdr QF

An armed fisheries protection vessel on the lines of a small warship with an armament of one or two small quick-firing guns and small arms. She had an impressive ram bow and was credited with 17 kts, but this is dubious, as she was less powerful than the similar *Canada*. However, she was a great improvement on the *Petrel*, which she replaced for Great Lakes fisheries patrol. Sold 1924, she was chartered by the Customs Preventive Service from 1927 to 1929 for East Coast patrols. The *Vigilant* was eventually converted to a barge and was not scrapped until 1956.

Canada. NAC PA206972

CANADA 1904-1924

Builder:	Vickers Sons and Maxim, Barrow-in-Furness, England
Date Completed:	1904
Tonnage:	411 (gross)
Dimensions:	200 x 25 x 10.5 (ft)
Machinery:	Twin screw steam triple expansion, 1800 IHP
Speed:	22 kts
Armament:	Four 3 pdr QF

A very effective little vessel used for naval training in the period before the Royal Canadian Navy was established as well as for fisheries patrols. In her first year of operation she was sent on a cruise to the West Indies with Naval Militia recruits embarked and she later provided sea training for the first officer cadets of the infant RCN. The maximum speed of 22 kts is in doubt: *Janes* for 1914 credits her with 17 kts. The *Canada* was transferred to the RCN in 1914 and commissioned as a patrol vessel. The foc'sle was raised and the peacetime armament of four 3 pdr QF was increased to two 12 pdr and two 3 pdr. Decommissioned November 1919. Sold (commercial) 1924 and reported lost off Florida in 1926.

Malaspina. BCA HP000519

GALIANO 1914-1918
MALASPINA 1914-1939

Builder:	Dublin Dockyard, Ireland
Date Completed:	1913
Tonnage:	392 (gross)
Dimensions:	162 x 27 x 13 (depth) (ft)
Machinery:	Single screw steam triple expansion, 1350 IHP
Speed:	14.5 kts

Purchased 1914 for fisheries protection duties in the Pacific. Taken over by the RCN, their wartime employment alternated between naval and civil duties. *Galiano* was wrecked in Barkley Sound in October 1918 while under naval control but *Malaspina* resumed fisheries protection duties in 1920. In 1939 she was again commissioned in the RCN as a patrol and examination vessel and later as a training ship. Paid off 1945 and scrapped 1946.

Arleux. Ken Macpherson (Private collection)

Arras. Ken Macpherson (Private collection).

ARLEUX 1919-1939
ARRAS 1919-1939
GIVENCHY 1919-1939

Builder:	Canadian Vickers, Montreal, QC
Date Completed:	1918/19
Tonnage:	357 (gross)
Dimensions:	130 x 25 x 13 (depth) (ft)
Machinery:	Single screw steam triple expansion, 480 IHP
Speed:	10 kts

These vessels were part of a class of about 45 Admiralty designed naval trawlers that proved to be very useful for peacetime duties. Some were retained by the RCN, others transferred to Fisheries and Marine and the remainder found ready purchasers in the fishing industry. These three examples were built by Canadian Vickers, Montreal and were identical to the buoy vessel *Loos*. They were employed as fisheries protection vessels, the first two in the Atlantic and *Givenchy* in the Pacific. All were returned to the RCN in 1939. *Arras* and *Arleux* became gate vessels, controlling the anti-submarine nets at Sydney and Halifax respectively. *Arleux* was sold (commercial) in 1946 and foundered off Nova Scotia in 1948. *Arras* was broken up in 1957. *Givenchy* was an accommodation ship on the West Coast and was sold in 1946. In naval service, they mounted one 12 pdr gun.

Givenchy. DFO

CHAPTER 7
HYDROGRAPHIC SURVEY SHIPS

Accurate hydrographic surveys are a requirement for safe navigation on any coast and, from the beginning of European settlement, Canadian authorities have endeavored to provide mariners with the means to navigate safely. Samuel de Champlain, who made his first voyage to North America in 1603, and became Lieutenant Governor of New France in 1633, was committed to mapping in detail the land and water of what is now eastern Canada. Throughout the seventeenth and early eighteenth centuries, French surveyors created and improved the charts. Jean Deshayes, who died at Quebec in 1706, raised chart making to a new degree of accuracy and by 1740 the Gulf of St. Lawrence was adequately charted for the purposes of trade and the requirements of the French Navy.

In 1758 James Cook, then Master of HMS *Pembroke,* started his surveying career. He was encouraged in this endeavour by his Captain, John Simcoe, father of John Graves Simcoe, the future first Lieutenant-Governor of Upper Canada. Cook carried out surveys of the St. Lawrence River for Admiral Saunders' fleet prior to the attack on Quebec City. He worked with Colonel Joseph des Barres, the noted land surveyor, and when the Treaty of Paris ended the Seven Years' War, Cook was assigned to conduct the hydrographic survey of Newfoundland. This took four years and resulted in charts that were still in use over a hundred years later. His Pacific voyages later took him to what is now British Columbia, essentially as an explorer, but he made numerous surveys there, putting his mark on both of Canada's oceanic coasts.

Henry Wolsey Bayfield is considered to be the father of hydrographic surveying in this country. From 1817 to 1856, he was the principal Royal Navy surveyor in Canada. From 1822 to 1825 he worked at charting Lake Erie, Lake Huron and Lake Superior. In 1827 he moved to Quebec City and spent fourteen years surveying the St. Lawrence before turning his attention to the East Coast. He also wrote the first Sailing Directions for the Gulf and River St. Lawrence and the Nova Scotia Pilot. He retired from surveying in 1856, settling in Charlottetown, PEI. Three survey vessels have borne his name.

After 1867 surveys in Canada became the responsibility of the Dominion government. It was not until 1883 that an intensive effort was made to complete the survey of the Great Lakes, starting with Georgian Bay. The Georgian Bay survey was headed by Staff Commander J.G. Boulton, on loan from the Admiralty but paid by the Dominion government. On the West Coast, the Royal Navy continued to be responsible for charting. In 1893, the Hydrographic Service of Canada was founded. Its first head was William J. Stewart (Chief Surveyor 1893-1925) who was succeeded by a succession of distinguished scientists and administrators. The Hydrographic Department was particularly prone to be switched from one government department to another, but quietly continued its work, issuing charts of the highest quality and accuracy.

Hydrographers often worked from land bases using small boats or were able to charter local vessels. In 1884, however, the Georgian Bay Survey did start with its own ship—a twenty year old tugboat renamed *Bayfield*. This vessel was the first of a line of ever more sophisticated hydrographic survey ships.

The schooners mentioned below were used by Cook and Bayfield. Another later vessel, the *Chrissie C. Thomey*, was a merchant schooner formerly in the Newfoundland to West Indies trade.

Grenville. Sketch by Marine Artist F.R. Berchem

GRENVILLE

GRENVILLE (1) 1763-1767

A small schooner built in Massachusetts, of 68 tons burden. She was used by James Cook and his two assistants to make his famous survey of Newfoundland. She would have been very much like the *Sultana*, built in Maryland in 1768, for which detailed plans (sufficient to build a replica) have survived. The illustration is based on the *Sultana*.

Gulnare. Sketch by Marine Artist F.R. Berchem

GULNARE

GULNARE (1) (2) & (3) 1828-c1856

Henry Bayfield had, in succession, three schooners built for the surveying service, all named *Gulnare* (for the heroine of Byron's poem "The Corsair"). The first was built in Quebec in 1828 and measured 140 tons burden. The artist's rendering represents the second vessel, of 180 tons burden, built by Peake and Duncan in Prince Edward Island in 1845. W. Stephenson of Quebec, probably acting as agent for the British Admiralty, is given as the owner. She was launched in May 1844 and was described in *The Royal Gazette* for 11 November 1845 as "...a beautiful copper fastened vessel of 180 tons burden.....intended for the surveying service and will be immediately placed under the command of Captain Bayfield, RN." In 1852 she was replaced by a third schooner of the same name.

CHRISSIE C. THOMEY 1910-1913

Built:	Burgeo, Nfld
Date Completed:	1908
Tonnage:	123 NRT
Dimensions:	102 x 26.7 x 10 (depth) (ft)
(Sail only)	

A fast wooden three-masted schooner purchased in 1910. In 1913, with winter approaching, she was trapped behind a sandbar at the mouth of the Rupert River in James Bay and, although undamaged, had to be abandoned.

Bayfield. Ron Beaupré (Private Collection)

BAYFIELD (1) 1884-1902

Built:	Buffalo, NY
Date Completed:	1864
Tonnage:	150 (gross)
Dimensions:	110 x 18 x 9 (depth) (ft)
Machinery:	Single screw steam simple, 75 NHP

The first ship purchased for the surveying service. She was a wooden tug, built as the *Edsal* and became the *Gen. US Grant* in 1872. Renamed in honour of Admiral Henry Bayfield who for forty years had been the Admiralty Surveyor in Canada, and charted much of the East Coast and the Great Lakes. Under the direction of Staff Commander George Boulton, the ship commenced work on the Georgian Bay survey in 1884, and also served in Lakes Superior and Erie. Comparison with an earlier image shows that her foc'sle had been raised since her purchase and her deckhouse modified. These major alterations also suggest that she had been re-boilered and probably given a compound engine. In 1901 she was in poor condition but remained in service until 1902 when replaced by the *Bayfield (2)*. Sold 1903.

Bayfield. Ron Beaupré (Private Collection)

BAYFIELD (2) 1902-1935

Builder:	D & W Henderson, Glasgow
Date Completed:	1889
Tonnage:	276 (gross)
Dimensions:	140 x 24 x 11 (depth) (ft)
Machinery:	Twin screw steam triple expansion, 160 NHP

A steel tug, formerly the *Lord Stanley*. Purchased 1901 to replace the first *Bayfield* on Great Lakes survey duties but was damaged in Toronto after refitting and did not start service until 1903. Sold 1935. Wrecked 1949 in Newfoundland.

Bayfield. NAC PA206960

98

LILLOOET 1907-1939

Builder:	BC Marine Railways, Esquimalt, BC
Date Completed:	1907
Tonnage:	575 (gross)
Dimensions:	140 x 24 x 11 (depth) (ft)
Machinery:	Twin screw steam triple expansion, 950 IHP
Speed:	13 kts

The first ship of the Canadian Hydrographic Service designed and built for hydrographic survey. A very successful ship, she could carry four or five small survey craft and had a total crew of 40, including six hydrographers. She was the only hydrographic ship on the West Coast but would tow "houseboats" with additional hydrographers and facilities. These craft were moored in protected inlets and acted as bases for the surveyors. The *Lillooet* was sold in 1939.

Cartier. DFO

Cartier. DFO

CARTIER (1) 1910-1939

Builder:	Swan Hunter at Newcastle, England
Date Completed:	1910
Tonnage:	556 (gross)
Dimensions:	164 x 29 x 13 (depth) (ft)
Machinery:	Twin screw steam triple expansion, 830 IHP
Speed:	12 kts

The *Cartier* was the East Coast equivalent to the *Lillooet*. A handsome ship built on yacht-like lines, her stem was decorated with the Canadian Coast of Arms and scroll work. The builder's model in Coast Guard headquarters shows her with bulwarks from the break of the foc'sle to the after end of the deckhouse but these were soon plated in—no doubt in response to Canadian weather conditions. The first photograph shows her with the sides partially enclosed and the second with plating extending nearly to the stern. The *Cartier* served as an armed patrol vessel in the RCN during the First World War and as a training ship in the Second World War. In December 1941 she was renamed *Charny*. Paid off December 1945, sold 1947 and scrapped at Sydney, NS.

SPEEDY II 1912-1921

Built:	Leith, Scotland
Date Completed:	1896
Tonnage:	252 (gross)
Dimensions:	115 x 21 x 10.6 (ft)
Machinery:	Single screw steam triple expansion, 88 NHP

A graceful former yacht, the *Speedy II* came to Canada in 1904 but was not registered here until 1912. Owned by the Department of Public Works and employed as a survey vessel on the Great Lakes. Sold 1921.

LA CANADIENNE (2) 1906-1918

Builder:	Robert Duncan at Port Glasgow, Scotland
Date Completed:	1880
Tonnage:	372 (gross)
Dimensions:	154 x 23 x 11 (depth) (ft)
Machinery:	(As re-engined) Single screw steam triple expansion, 60 NHP

An iron vessel, built as the *Foxhound*. Originally a fisheries patrol vessel, in 1906 she was transferred to the hydrographic service for work on the St. Lawrence and Great Lakes. Laid up 1918 and scrapped 1920.

A second specially designed survey vessel for the East Coast, the *Acadia* served as a hydrographic ship for fifty-six years, interrupted by interludes in naval service. The *Acadia's* bow was embellished with the arms of Ontario and Nova Scotia on the starboard side and of Quebec and New Brunswick to port. They were carved from wood and were destroyed when a shed in which they were stored burnt down while the ship was being refitted in Pictou, NS, in the 1950s. The *Acadia* was the first ship in the hydrographic fleet to be fitted with Marconi wireless telegraphy. In the First World War, she was requisitioned by the RCN and commissioned as an antisubmarine patrol vessel from January 1917 to March 1919. She received a Sperry gyro compass in 1928 and a deep-sea echo sounder in 1929. In 1939, she was again taken up by the Navy, serving as a patrol craft and as a gunnery training ship. Her armament in this role was one 4-inch gun and one 12 pdr. Reverting to hydrographic service, she surveyed the Newfoundland coast after confederation with Canada in 1949. In 1955 she received a new bridge, but remained a coal burner throughout her career. The *Acadia* retired in 1969 and is preserved at the Maritime Museum of the Atlantic at Halifax, NS where she is open to the public.

ACADIA (2) 1913-1969

Builder:	Swan Hunter at Newcastle, England
Date Completed:	1913
Tonnage:	846 (gross)
Dimensions:	182.5 x 34 x 13 (depth) (ft)
Machinery:	Single screw steam triple expansion, 1200 IHP
Speed:	12 kts

STADACONA 1920-1924

Builder:	Cramp, Philadelphia, PA
Date Completed:	1893
Tonnage:	780 (gross)
Dimensions:	168 x 30.5 x 16 (depth) (ft)
Machinery:	Single screw steam triple expansion, 99 NHP

An iron vessel built as a yacht. Her original name was *Columbia*. She was purchased by the RCN in 1915 for use as a patrol craft at Halifax (the photo shows her in naval service wearing a white ensign). In 1919 she was transferred to the West Coast and was employed as a hydrographic survey vessel, and occasionally on fisheries patrol, until she was sold in 1924. She was subsequently a rum runner, a yacht and finally a towboat. Scrapped at Seattle in 1948.

Wm. J. STEWART 1932-1975

Builder:	Collingwood Shipyards, ON
Date Completed:	1932
Tonnage:	1295 (gross)
Dimensions:	228 x 36 x 11.5 (ft)
Machinery:	Twin screw steam triple expansion, 1200 IHP
Speed:	12 kts

As the *Lillooet* was aging, a larger survey vessel was ordered for service on the Pacific coast. The *Wm. J. Stewart* was named for the first head of the Canadian Hydrographic Survey, William James Stewart (Chief Hydrographer 1893-1925). She was a superior vessel and the pride of the service. During the Second World War, when her East Coast sisters were commandeered by the RCN, she continued her survey work. In 1944 the *Stewart* struck the notorious Ripple Rock in Seymour Narrows, between Vancouver Island and the mainland. She sank in shallow water in Plumper Bay but was salvaged, repaired and refitted by the summer of 1945. In 1958, Ripple Rock was leveled and removed as a navigation hazard by the largest non-nuclear man made explosion to that time. The *Wm. J. Stewart* was retired in 1975 and became a restaurant vessel at Ucluelet, BC.

CHAPTER 8

MISCELLANEOUS TYPES

There has always been a need for specialized vessels and tugs, especially in the St. Lawrence ship channel and the canals and waterways leading to and between the Great Lakes. The "relief of wrecks" was part of F. Bâby's contract in the early days and from 1902 to 1952, the department responsible kept a salvage vessel available. The survey and sounding vessels were for checking the channels, not for initial hydrographic surveys, as were the ships listed in the previous chapter. Tugs were needed for moving dredges and barges about and for general duties. Lightships were important aids to navigation and were stationed at the entrance to important harbours and channels and to mark dangerous offshore shoals. In addition to the light, they sounded a powerful foghorn during periods of restricted visibility and, when radio direction finding was introduced, they were fitted with radio beacons. This could be dangerous for the lightship crew—in foggy conditions ships would home in on the beacon and sometimes would not see the lightship until it was too late to avoid collision. Canadian lightships, although experiencing many close calls, were fortunate in being spared serious disaster.

Salvage vessels

LORD STRATHCONA 1902-1947

Builder:	J.P. Rennoldson, South Shields, England
Date Completed:	1902
Tonnage:	495 (gross)
Dimensions:	160 x 27 x 13.5 (depth) (ft)
Machinery:	Twin screw steam triple expansion, 250 NHP

A steel salvage vessel, essentially a powerful tug with additional deck space. Broken up in 1947.

TRAVERSE 1930-1952

Builder:	George Brown, Greenock, Scotland
Date Completed:	1930
Tonnage:	317 (gross)
Dimensions:	130 x 26 x 10.5 (depth) (ft)
Machinery:	Single screw diesel, 227 NHP

A steel salvage vessel. Sold 1952. Scrapped 1966.

Bellechasse. DFO

Sounding and Survey vessels

BELLECHASSE 1912-1942

Builder:	Kingston Shipbuilding, Kingston, ON
Date Completed:	1912
Tonnage:	417 (gross)
Dimensions:	130 x 27 (ft)
Machinery:	Twin screw steam triple expansion, 1000 IHP
Speed:	13 kts

A steel survey and inspection vessel for the St. Lawrence Ship Channel. Retired 1948 and broken up in 1954.

Detector. DFO

DETECTOR

1915-1978

Built:	Canadian Government Shipyard, QC
Date Completed:	1915
Tonnage:	584 (gross)
Dimensions:	147 x 35 x 10 (ft)
Machinery:	Twin screw steam compound, 532 IHP
Speed:	10 kts

The *Detector* was specially concerned with the maintenance of the statutory depth of water in the St. Lawrence Ship Channel and "swept the channel" by towing a bar at a given depth. She was the oldest and longest serving vessel in the government service when sold in 1978.

Berthier. DFO

BERTHIER

1916-1961

Built:	Canadian Government Shipyard, QC
Date Completed:	1916
Tonnage:	368 (gross)
Dimensions:	128 x 24 x 8 (ft)
Machinery:	Single screw steam triple expansion, 550 IH
Speed:	10.5 kts

A survey and inspection vessel for the St. Lawrence Ship Channel. Sold 1961.

LANORAIE II

1928-1956

Built:	Canadian Government Shipyard, Sorel, QC
Date Completed:	1928
Tonnage:	177 (gross)
Dimensions:	94 x 23 x 10 (ft)
Machinery:	Single screw compound 336 IHP
Speed:	10 kts

A survey and inspection vessel for the St. Lawrence Ship Channel. Sold (commercial) 1956.

FRONTENAC

1930-1968

Built:	Canadian Government Shipyard, Sorel, QC
Date Completed:	1930
Tonnage:	248 (gross)
Dimensions:	109 x 24 x 10 (ft)
Machinery:	Single screw triple expansion 472 IHP
Speed:	10 kts

A survey and inspection vessel for the St. Lawrence Ship Channel. Out of service and abandoned 1968.

Lanoraie II. DFO

Frontenac. DFO

James Howden. NAC PA52680

Murray Stewart. Ron Beaupré (Private Collection)

Jalobert. DFO

Tugs

JAMES HOWDEN 1903-1929

Built:	Canadian Government Shipyard, Sorel, QC
Date Completed:	1903
Tonnage:	177 (gross)
Dimensions:	100 x 21 x 7.5 (ft)
Machinery:	Steam compound, 44 NHP

An example of a typical tug of the period. Dismantled 1929.

MURRAY STEWART 1922-1939

Builder:	Port Arthur Shipbuilding, ON
Date Completed:	1918
Tonnage:	234 (gross)
Dimensions:	109 x 26 x 16 (ft)
Machinery:	Single screw steam triple expansion, 156 NHP
Speed:	10 kts

A steel tug, purchased 1922 for use on the Great Lakes and typical of a number of tugs that were employed in the St. Lawrence Ship Channel and inland waterways. Served with the RCN 1939-1946. Sold (commercial) 1946.

JALOBERT 1923-1954

Builder:	Kingston Shipbuilding, Kingston, ON
Date Completed:	1911
Tonnage:	278 (gross)
Dimensions:	107.5 x 23 x 12 (depth) (ft)
Machinery:	Single screw steam compound, 120 NHP
Speed:	11 kts

A steel tug, built as the *Polana* for the Department of Agriculture. Transferred to Marine and Fisheries and renamed *Jalobert* in 1923. From 1939 to 1945 she was used as the Pilot Vessel at Rimouski and for Naval Control of Shipping. Sold (commercial) 1954; became *Macassar* 1954 and *Queen City* 1965. Floating restaurant 1980.

NOTE: These three tugs are included as representatives of a fairly numerous class of hardworking craft. The following two vessels were larger and different in purpose and design.

CITADELLE

1932-1952

Builder:	Davie Shipbuilding, Lévis, QC
Date Completed:	1932
Tonnage:	431 (gross)
Dimensions:	120.5 x 30 x 13.5 (depth) (ft)
Machinery:	Single screw steam triple expansion, 105 NHP

A steel fire-fighting tug. Stationed at Quebec City and employed on a variety of duties. Converted for use as the Pilot Vessel at Rimouski, replacing *Jalobert*. Sold 1962. Scrapped 1966.

OCEAN EAGLE

1938-1946

Builder:	Day, Summers & Co, Southampton, England
Date Completed:	1919
Tonnage:	420 (gross)
Dimensions:	135 X 29 x 14 (depth) (ft)
Machinery:	Single screw steam triple expansion, 116 NHP

A Saint class tug, formerly the *St. Arvans*, sister to the *Franklin (1)* and *St. Heliers*. Purchased in 1927 for the Department of Railways and Canals. Transferred to the National Harbours Board and later to the Department of Transport in 1938. Sold (commercial) in 1946. Renamed *Aigle d'Ocean*. Lost in tragic circumstances in Hudson Strait in 1975, some crew members being saved by CCGS *Norman McLeod Rogers*.

Lightships

LIGHTSHIP No. 7

No.7 is typical of late 19th century lightships. She is wooden and schooner rigged. The light, fuelled by whale oil, is hoisted to the triatic stay between the masts. The boiler is not for propulsion but to power the steam foghorn, which is seen just aft of the funnel (the steam foghorn was invented by Robert Foulis for whom a ship was later named). The name of the station is normally painted on the side but is not seen here—perhaps she is a relief vessel.

LIGHTSHIP No. 20

This ship was built for the RCN as the Battle class trawler *St. Eloi*. In 1920 nine of these useful vessels were turned over to the Department of Marine and Fisheries. One was soon returned to the RCN, *Loos* became a buoy tender, *Arleux, Arras* and *Givenchy* were used as fisheries patrol vessels and four were converted to lightships (No. 3, ex *Messines,* No. 5, ex *Vimy,* No. 20, ex *St. Eloi* and No. 22, ex *St. Julien*). The light, now electric, is at the foremast head and the foghorn is on the latticework tower. Note the radio aerials. No. 20 is typical of lightships between the wars.

Lightship No. 7. DFO

Lightship No. 20. DFO

Non-Government Northern Supply Vessels

BEOTHIC Chartered 1927

Builder: American Steamboat Company, Lorraine, OH
Tonnage: 2018 (gross)

UNGAVA Under contract 1932

Builder: Detroit Shipbuilding Co, Wyandotte, MI
Tonnage: 1914 (gross)

Specifications for all above:

Date Completed: 1918
Dimensions: 262.5 x 43.7 x 18.4 (ft)
Machinery: Single screw steam triple expansion, 274 NHP

These ships were both First World War standard small freighters, originally ordered by the British Government as *War Wren* and *War Hope*, but taken over by the US Shipping Board and launched as *Lake Como* and *Lake Butler*. In 1925, Job Bros of St. John's Newfoundland purchased the *Lake Como* for use as a sealer and coastal freighter. She was lengthened, strengthened for ice and renamed *Beothic*. In 1927 she was chartered by the Canadian Government for the Arctic Expedition and Eastern Arctic patrol. The *Ungava*, ex *Palatka*, ex *Lake Butler*, was bought by Job Bros in 1928 and similarly modified. In 1932 she was bareboat chartered to the Hudson Bay Company for a northern resupply voyage with the Canadian government reserving space on board.

Nascopie. DFO

NASCOPIE Under contract 1933-1947

Builder:	Swan Hunter & Wigham Richardson, Newcastle
Date Completed:	1912
Tonnage:	2521 (gross)
Dimensions:	285.5 x 43.8 x 20.2 (depth) (ft)
Machinery:	Single screw steam triple expansion, 339 NHP

The *Nascopie* was an effective icebreaker built as a supply vessel for the Hudson Bay Company's Arctic posts. For most of its service the *Nascopie* was commanded by Captain R. Smellie, an expert Arctic hand and ice master. In 1930 she was laid up due to the world financial slump, but in 1933 she was refitted and her passenger accommodation increased. Her base of operations was changed from England to Montreal and, although operated by the Hudson Bay Company, passenger and cargo space was reserved for the RCMP and other government Departments. From 1933 to 1947 she effectively carried out the Eastern Arctic Patrol, later conducted by the *C.D. Howe*. In 1937 she established a post (Fort Ross) at Bellott Strait and there met the Hudson Bay Company schooner *Aklavik* from the Western Arctic. The two ships returned to their respective bases but Captain Gall of the *Aklavik* transferred to the *Nascopie* and became the first person to travel the Northwest Passage from west to east. The *Nascopie's* last trip came two years after Captain Smellie had retired. On her 1947 voyage she struck a reef near Cape Dorset, Baffin Island and became a total loss.

PART 2 1946–2000

INTRODUCTION

Even before the United States became involved in the Second World War, President Roosevelt and Prime Minister Mackenzie King met in Ogdensburg, New York, in 1940 and established a framework for Canadian and United States cooperation in the defence of the North American continent. Under the Ogdensburg Agreement, airfields, radio and air navigation facilities were built in the Canadian north to facilitate air traffic and the flow of military supplies to the European theatre and, from 1941, to the Soviet Union. This activity continued after the war in the late 1940s, especially in the eastern Arctic where joint US/Canadian radio and meteorological stations continued to be established. Canada supplied the locales for the bases and some personnel, but in the immediate post-war period, Canada was simply not capable of undertaking major projects in the Arctic. When a base was established at Resolute on Cornwallis Island in 1947, the shipping used was entirely American, including USN and USCG icebreakers.

It was apparent that unless we could provide an effective sea lift capability and icebreakers to support it, the Arctic archipelago would be effectively under American control. This became even more evident with the onset of the Cold War. Northern military installations became vital to the security of the North American continent and it was clear that, in order to maintain its sovereignty as well as meet Canadian defence commitments, Canada had to participate fully in the construction and re-supply of the Distant Early Warning radar sites and other military establishments in the north. The Canadian government also intended to facilitate exploration for Arctic resources and to improve the living standards of the Inuit, (although some of the ways in which this was done would have mixed or negative results). To carry out these programs, a patrol, hospital and service ship, the *C.D. Howe*, and new large icebreakers, the *D'Iberville* being the first, were built for the Department of Transport. The RCN had its own icebreaker, the *Labrador*. Special supply vessels were converted from wartime landing craft, and smaller ice-capable ships were added to the fleet.

These developments in the Arctic, both economic and for defence purposes, together with increases in trade and shipping along the already existing routes, resulted in the transformation of the Department of Transport's Marine Services fleet from a series of regional units under local control to an organization that could act as an instrument of national policy. This change was manifested by the creation of the Canadian Coast Guard in January 1962. Between 1950 and 1970, over twenty major ships, five of which were powerful icebreakers, were added to the fleet along with many smaller vessels. From 1978 to 1988, a Fleet Capital Investment Plan resulted in a second spurt of construction or purchase of major ships to replace vessels built under earlier programs. These included five icebreakers, but a long-term initiative to build a truly Arctic icebreaker (known as the Polar 8) capable of year-round operation was finally canceled in 1990.

Another area of postwar fleet expansion was in the field of Search and Rescue. Overall responsibility for the organization was given to the Department of National Defence. The Air Force supplied the aircraft and helicopters but the Coast Guard provided the seaborne element, from station based lifeboats to offshore cutters. After the wreck of the tanker *Arrow* off Cape Breton in 1970, countering the threat of oil pollution by wrecked tankers also became an important task for the Coast Guard. Specialized small craft were developed for the purpose, while all major ships carried oil spill booms and clean-up equipment.

After the war, the Canadian Hydrographic Service temporarily replaced old and worn out ships with ex-Navy vessels and then built a new fleet of modern survey and science vessels, including two large ice-strengthened ships suited to hydrographic and oceanographic work in the Arctic. The Fisheries Research Board, established in 1937, employed a number of research trawlers and also carried out oceanographic research that was broader in scope. In 1961 fisheries and oceanographic research as well as hydrographic survey were consolidated in the Marine Sciences Branch of the Department of Mines and Technical Surveys.

Fisheries enforcement requirements in the immediate postwar period were practically the same as before 1939, but in July 1964 Canada increased its territorial sea limits from three miles to twelve. In January 1977 a two-hundred-mile exclusive economic zone was proclaimed. These changes required fisheries patrol vessels for work offshore as well as coastal and inshore craft.

In 1995, as a measure to rationalize administration, combine tasks, reduce the number of ships and save money, the Coast Guard was put under the administration of the Department of Fisheries and Oceans and the two government fleets were amalgamated. The wheel had turned full circle to the arrangement begun in 1867.

Administrative changes since the Second World War.

1946	Ships requisitioned by the Navy are returned to civilian operation, but most are worn out and are temporarily replaced by former naval vessels. The Canadian Naval Auxiliary Service is formed.
1949	The Marine Division of the RCMP is established with a fleet composed initially of former naval vessels.
	The Department of Mines and Resources, which includes the Canadian Hydrographic Service, becomes the Department of Mines and Technical Surveys.
1961	As oceanographic research becomes more important, the Department of Mines and Technical Surveys forms a Marine Sciences branch with the responsibility of fisheries and oceanographic research and hydrographic survey.
1962	The Canadian Marine Service fleet of the Department of Transport becomes the Canadian Coast Guard.
1970	The Marine Division of the RCMP is disbanded and regional divisions take over responsibility for marine matters.
1971	Fisheries becomes part of the newly formed Department of the Environment, which also takes over the Marine Sciences branch. The hydrographic and oceanographic ships and the fisheries vessels continue to serve their respective branches. It is renamed the Department of Fisheries and the Environment in 1976.
1979	The Department of Fisheries and the Environment splits into Environment Canada and the Department of Fisheries and Oceans. DFO's fleet comprises hydrographic and oceanographic, fisheries research and fisheries enforcement vessels.
1995	The Coast Guard, except for its regulatory functions, is transferred from the Department of Transport to the Department of Fisheries and Oceans and the two fleets are amalgamated. This once again brings all the federal government's civilian manned ships, except for naval auxiliaries, under the administration of a single department

Colour schemes of ships in Part 2

Until 1995 hydrographic and oceanographic research vessels were white with buff funnels, the traditional colours for scientific vessels. Fisheries patrol vessels were gray— a somewhat darker shade than the ships of the RCN. From the mid-sixties, the crest of the Fisheries Conservation and Protection Branch was mounted on each side of the funnel. Fisheries research craft usually had black hulls, but in 1990 this was changed to white like other research ships. RCMP Marine Division vessels had dark blue-gray hulls and funnel tops with lighter grey superstructure. The letters MP and a hull number were displayed forward on the hull and on the transom with the RCMP crest on the funnel or other prominent position. Naval Auxiliary vessels have dark gray hulls, medium gray upperworks and gray funnels with a black top.

Before the Canadian Coast Guard was created in 1962, the ships of the Marine Service of the Department of Transport had black hulls, white bulwarks and upperworks, buff masts and buff funnels with black tops. The new Coast Guard livery was a red hull, white bulwarks and superstructure and white funnels with a red maple leaf and red band. The upper part of the funnel was black and masts and derricks remained buff. There would be several changes to this over the years. In 1975 a white diagonal slash was added on which was centered a red bar and maple leaf and the words COAST GUARD and GARDE CÔTIÈRE in large white letters painted forward and aft of the slash. In 1984 a new Federal Identity program was put in place and a new overall red colour, more towards the orange end of the spectrum, was adopted. Bulwarks, formerly white, were now painted red. The slash was moved forward on the hull and COAST GUARD and GARDE CÔTIÈRE appeared in smaller letters located aft of the slash. The Canada word-mark was added near the stern. The red band was removed from the funnel, leaving only the maple leaf and the black top was made much narrower. Dedicated Search and Rescue vessels were differentiated by yellow superstructures for better visibility and identification. Finally, in 1995, the Coast Guard was transferred to the Department of Fisheries and Oceans and the fleets were combined. Various colour schemes were considered for the former DFO ships, like adding red slashes to the gray hulls of the fisheries patrol vessels and the white scientific ships. All would have had the same funnel insignia. In the end, all ships, regardless of employment, adopted the same Coast Guard colours. The Canada word-mark was removed from the hull and placed on the superstructure and a Fisheries and Oceans logo replaced it on the hull. It is possible to identify the period in which a photo of a Coast Guard ship was taken by closely examining its paint scheme, always allowing for the fact that colours were often not changed until the ship completed its next scheduled refit.

The icebreaker *Louis S. St. Laurent* at Halifax. DFO

The icebreaker *John A. Macdonald* at Quebec. DFO

The icebreaker *D'Iberville* working in the St. Lawrence River. DFO

The icebreaker *Pierre Radisson* escorting a tanker. DFO

Light icebreaker *Ann Harvey* with the Hibernia oil platform. DFO

The veteran icebreaker *N.B. McLean*. DFO

The northern supply vessel *Skua*, a former landing craft. DFO

The small buoy tender *Verendrye* in the Ottawa River. DFO

A shallow draft navigation aids vessel, the first *Eckaloo*, in the Mackenzie River.

The weather ship *Quadra*. DFO

The survey vessel *Ville Marie*. DFO

The icebreakers *Ernest Lapointe* and *D'Iberville* escorting a freighter near Trois Rivières. Painting by Yves Bérubé.

SAR Cutter *Gordon Reid.* DFO

The Arun class self-righting lifeboat *Bickerton*. DFO

The hovercraft *Siyäy*. *Vancouver Sun*

The hovercraft *Voyageur* with a deck cargo. DFO

The research trawler *G.B. Reed.* DFO

The ice-strengthened oceanographic and hydrographic ship *Hudson*. DFO

The hydrographic survey vessel *Wm. J. Stewart*. DFO

The hydrographic survey vessel *Acadia* preserved at the Maritime Museum of the Atlantic, Halifax. DFO

Opposite top: The RCMP patrol vessel *Wood* which became the SAR cutter *Daring*. DFO

Opposite bottom: The fisheries patrol vessel *Howay*, formerly the RCMP vessel *Macdonald*. DFO

Above: The naval auxiliary tugs *Glenevis*, *Firebird* and *Merrikville* at Halifax. MCM

Governor-General's Honorary Flag

Canadian Coast Guard Vessel Jack

Flags & Pennants

Minister's Flag

Deputy Minister's Flag

Canadian Coast Guard Commissioner's Flag

Canadian Coast Guard Deputy Commisionner's Flag

Canadian Coast Guard Fleet Director General's Pennant

Canadian Coast Guard Senior Officer's Pennant

Canadian Coast Guard Auxiliary Services Pennant

Fisheries Patrol Vessel Pennant

Canadian Hydrographic Services Flag

Crests

Left to right: Canadian Coast Guard; Fisheries Patrol Service; Canadian Hydrographic Service; Canadian Naval Auxiliary Service; Royal Canadian Mounted Police.

144

CHAPTER 9

THE EASTERN ARCTIC PATROL SHIP

In the postwar period, it was apparent that a visible and effective Canadian presence in the Arctic was necessary to maintain our sovereignty in the remote Regions of the north. The second major ship of the postwar building program (the first was the ice-strengthened buoy tender *Edward Cornwallis*) was designed and constructed as a multi-purpose patrol vessel for the eastern Arctic. The *C.D. Howe* represented a continuation of the policy that sent the *Neptune* north in 1903 and of Captain Bernier's patrols with the *Arctic* from 1904 to 1926. The chartered *Beothic* and *Nascopie* had, to some extent, filled the gap until the Second World War, when the *St. Roch* made her epic voyage.

From 1950 to 1970, the *C.D. Howe* made annual voyages to northern Labrador and the south and east coasts of Baffin Island, stopping at every coastal settlement and station and also at points on Ellesmere Island. There was accommodation for eighty-eight passengers as well as a crew of fifty-eight. She carried Department of Northern Affairs, National Resources employees and RCMP members. Navigation aids were activated for the season and relief meteorological personnel were brought to their stations. Cargo and supplies were landed at all stops. The provision of medical and dental services were probably her most important roles. She had a well-equipped hospital and carried two doctors, two nurses, and one or two dentists. She was the first DOT ship to be equipped with a helicopter deck and to carry a helicopter.

In 1953 *C.D. Howe* carried Inuit families, with their sled dog, kayaks and other posessions, from Inukjuag (then called Port Harrison) on the eastern side of Hudson Bay, to

Craig Harbour on Ellesmere Island, later changed to Grise Fjord which had easier access for supply vessels; and in 1955 to Resolute on Cornwallis Island. The objective was to provide new hunting grounds and to populate some of the more northerly locations in the archipelago.

The *C.D. Howe* became redundant when better air communication to virtually all settlements became available, but it is interesting to note that when the Polar 8 icebreaker project was under development (project cancelled in 1990—see Chapter 10) it was envisaged that she would perform many of the same roles on a year-round basis and throughout the entire Arctic archipelago.

C.D. Howe. DFO

C.D. HOWE 1950-1970

Builder:	Davie Shipbuilding Ltd, Lauzon, QC
Date Completed:	1950
Tonnage:	3628 (gross)
Dimensions:	295 x 50 x 19.5 (ft) 91 x 15.4 x 6 (m)
Machinery:	Twin screw steam unaflow, 4000 IHP
Speed:	13.5 kts

A unique ice-strengthened Northern Service vessel named for the former Minister of Transport and wartime Minister of Munitions and Supplies. She was fitted with a helicopter deck and had a hangar added later. The *C.D. Howe* was employed on the Eastern Arctic Patrol and performed exemplary service in the north for twenty years and assisted shipping in the Gulf in winter. In her last years she also acted as a training vessel for Coast Guard College cadets. Sold 1970 and converted to an accommodation ship for workers at the Black Angel Mine in Maarmorilik Fjord, Greenland.

CHAPTER 10

THE POSTWAR ICEBREAKERS

P ostwar developments in the North, both economic and defence related, required large and powerful ships capable of operating in the high Arctic; but at the end of the Second World War, our best icebreaker was the seventeen-year-old *N.B. McLean* which was fully occupied on the Hudson Strait and Hudson Bay route during the navigation season. As the policy of the Canadian government was to participate fully in the construction of the Distant Early Warning radar line and other joint Canadian and United States military stations, a new icebreaker fleet, as well as other specialized vessels, would be needed. The first of the new large icebreakers would be the *D'Iberville*, completed in 1952.

The Royal Canadian Navy also became interested in the Arctic and commissioned HMCS *Labrador* in July 1954. Under Captains O.C.S. Robertson and T.C. Pullen, she performed valuable pioneering and exploratory work in the Arctic. On her first deployment in 1954 she became the first large ship to transit the Northwest Passage, via Viscount Melville Sound, Prince of Wales Strait and Amundsen Gulf, continuing on to become the first ship to circumnavigate North America in one season. After three seasons, to the disappointment of her crew and of an element at Naval Headquarters that felt that the Arctic was a proper area of interest to the Navy, she was transferred to Transport Canada so that the RCN could concentrate on anti-submarine warfare under the NATO mandate.

The icebreakers *John A. Macdonald, Louis S. St. Laurent* and *Norman McLeod Rogers* followed the *D'Iberville*. In addition, eight navigation aids vessels that were also classed as light icebreakers were added to the fleet. These ships were larger and more powerful than the existing small icebreakers *Saurel* and *Ernest Lapointe*. They could cover the Hudson Strait route and the lower latitudes in the eastern Arctic, and the western Arctic as well, though not without some damage on several occasions (they are listed in Chapter 13 under the heading of Navigation Aids vessels, their prime function). The existence of a powerful icebreaker fleet made it possible to extend the shipping season in the St. Lawrence River and Gulf to a year-round operation. This resulted in new traffic patterns: the Maritime ports lost much of the cargo that had moved through Saint John NB and Halifax in the winter months.

The next impetus for icebreaker design, though not in the end resulting in new construction, was stimulated by the voyage of the icebreaking tanker *Manhattan*, escorted by the *John A. Macdonald*, in 1969. The purpose was to explore the possibility of exporting oil from Alaska via the Northwest Passage to markets on the eastern seaboard. Studies for the design of a Canadian Polar icebreaker started shortly afterwards and for twenty years exercised the talents of Coast Guard engineering and design staff, only to be canceled in 1990. Eventually, Alaskan north-slope oil was transported, not by tanker, but by pipeline to Valdez in southern Alaska, and thence by tanker to the US West Coast.

When offshore oil exploration in the Beaufort Sea started in the mid-seventies, the companies concerned developed many ingenious platforms and techniques for working in an Arctic environment. As well as special drilling platforms and ships, they constructed their own icebreakers to novel designs. When Beaufort Sea development came to a halt in the 1980s, these very effective Canadian ships were dispersed, with the exception of the *Terry Fox*, which was eventually purchased by the Coast Guard.

Under the Fleet Capital Investment Plan, which was instituted in 1977, the older icebreakers were replaced by four new ships, classed as Type 1200 vessels: *Pierre Radisson, Sir John Franklin, Des Groseilliers* and *Henry Larsen*; while the largest icebreaker, the *Louis S. St. Laurent*, was extensively refitted. These full icebreakers were assisted by eight new combined light icebreaker / navigation aids vessels, assigned Type numbers 1100 and 1050, which were larger and more powerful than their predecessors.

In the last years of the twentieth century, milder conditions in the Arctic resulted in less need for icebreaker support, thereby freeing up some ship time to support Canadian and international scientific missions. Since 1988 no new major icebreaker has been constructed in Canada.

D'Iberville. DFO

D'IBERVILLE 1952-1983

Builder:	Davie Shipbuilding Ltd, Lauzon, QC
Date Completed:	1952
Tonnage:	5678 (gross)
Dimensions:	310 x 67 x 3 (ft) 94.5 x 20 x 9.1 (m)
Machinery:	Twin screw steam unaflow, 10800 IHP
Speed:	15 kts

The first of the large postwar icebreakers, designed by Milne, Gilmore and German. She was fitted with a flight deck and a hangar for two helicopters. Her two six cylinder Skinner unaflow engines, built at Montreal by Vickers, were the largest of the type in the Coast Guard. The valve arrangement in a unaflow recip-

rocating engine is somewhat like a two-stroke diesel: the cylinders are all of the same size and the exhaust steam is partially recompressed and used with new steam on the next stroke.

In June 1953 after completing her trials, the *D'Iberville* steamed directly to England to represent Canada at Queen Elizabeth II's coronation review, along with HMCS *Magnificent* and other ships of the RCN. On her first Arctic voyage, she established an RCMP post at Alexandria Fjord on Ellesmere Island, within 800 nautical miles of the Pole. The *D'Iberville* was based in the Quebec agency. She made annual trips to the Arctic and worked in the Gulf each winter. In 1983 this popular ship was decommissioned and laid up, first at Quebec, then at Sorel, but it was 1989 before she was sold for scrap.

LABRADOR 1958-1987

Builder:	Marine Industries Ltd, Sorel, QC
Date Completed:	1953
Tonnage:	3823 (gross)
Dimensions:	250 x 64 x 29 (ft) 76.2 x 19.5 x 8.8 (m)
Machinery:	Twin screw diesel-electric. 10000 SHP (7460 kW)
Speed:	16 kts

In the early 1950s, the Royal Canadian Navy decided to establish a presence in the Arctic and ordered an icebreaker for naval service. HMCS *Labrador* was a diesel-electric ship, practically identical to the Wind class icebreakers of the United States Coast Guard. In February 1958 she was transferred from the RCN to the Department of Transport and then carried out the normal duties of a Coast Guard icebreaker, deploying to the Arctic every year, including far northern voyages to Eureka and Alexandria Fjord. From 1977 she was employed chiefly on hydrographic surveys and in her last years, because of metal fatigue, was restricted to survey and scientific work in the lower latitudes while continuing to work in the Gulf in the winter. She was always based at Dartmouth, NS. Sold in 1987, replaced by the *Henry Larsen.*

John A. Macdonald. DFO

JOHN A. MACDONALD 1960-1991

Builder:	Davie Shipbuilding Ltd, Lauzon, QC
Date Completed:	1960
Tonnage:	6186 (gross)
Dimensions:	315 x 70 x 28.2 (ft) 97.2 x 21.3 x 8.6 (m)
Machinery:	Triple screw diesel-electric. 15000 SHP (11190 kW)
Speed:	15.5 kts

The *John A. Macdonald* was always a favoured ship and was considered by icebreaker crews to be the finest Coast Guard ice-breaker, before or since. The diesel-electric triple screw arrangement was ideal: the middle screw was deep and nearly immune to ice damage. The *John A. Macdonald* set many records. In 1967 she went through the Northwest Passage to assist the light icebreaker

Camsell in the Western Arctic and then went to the assistance of the USCGC *Northwind*, which was stuck in heavy ice north of Point Barrow, Alaska. After freeing the *Northwind*, she returned to Halifax via the Panama Canal, circumnavigating North America. In 1969 she transited the Passage in both directions, escorting the tanker *Manhattan* on her historic voyage. In 1975 she again went through to the western Arctic to assist the *Camsell* which had been damaged. In 1978-79 she was chartered to Dome Petroleum for one year and spent the winter in the Arctic. In 1985, she escorted the new USCG icebreaker *Polar Sea* in a transit that received much press coverage because of sovereignty implications. The *John A. Macdonald* was decommissioned in 1991 and sold in 1993. Replaced by the purchased *Terry Fox*.

LOUIS S. St. LAURENT 1969

Builder:	Canadian Vickers Ltd, Montreal, QC
Date Completed:	1969
Tonnage:	10908 (gross)
Dimensions:	366.5 x 80 x 31 (ft) 113 x 24.6 x 9.6 (m) (As built)
Machinery:	Triple screw steam turbo-electric, 27000 SHP (20142 kW)
Speed:	17.5 kts

As rebuilt at Halifax Shipyard, 1988-93

Tonnage:	11441 (gross)
Dimensions:	392 x 80 x 32 (ft) 119.6 x 24.6 x 9.9 (m) (as refitted)
Machinery:	Triple screw diesel-electric, 27000 SHP (20142 kW)
Speed:	17.5 kts

Louis S. St. Laurent. DFO

Louis S. St. Laurent. MB Mackay (Private Collection)

The largest ship ever built for the Canadian Coast Guard. When the construction of a very large icebreaker for the Coast Guard was proposed, nuclear propulsion was seriously being considered for merchant ships as well as for warships. The United States had built the nuclear-powered freighter *Savannah* and a West German ship was also completed. Such vessels are steam ships: the nuclear plant replaces the usual oil fired boilers. To gain experience in a high-powered turbine system with ultimate electric drive, a turbo-electric plant was specified, with the idea that progression to a nuclear system in the future would be less difficult. The *Louis S. St. Laurent* was thus saddled with very uneconomical machinery. Although our most powerful icebreaker, she only had enough fuel for about ten days of high-powered operation in ice before refuelling. Nevertheless, she did excellent work. She escorted the *Manhattan* during her second year of ice trials in 1970. The following year, on a joint Canadian and Danish scientific expedition, she went through the Robeson Channel between Ellesmere Island and Greenland and into the Lincoln Sea, reaching 82°56' North, the farthest by a western ship at that time.

In 1988 the *Louis S. St. Laurent* was taken in hand for a major overhaul which became a virtual rebuilding. The ship was gutted and the inner plating renewed. She received a new bow of improved design with an air bubbling system. The turbines were replaced by diesel engines with new generators and the three elec-

tric propulsion motors were rebuilt. The refit was very protracted and subject to unforeseen and expensive delays, but the ultimate result was a more capable ship with far greater endurance and economy. In 1994 the ship accompanied USCGC *Polar Sea* through the Bering Strait on a joint scientific expedition to the North Pole. There they met the Russian nuclear-powered icebreaker *Yamal*. As the *Polar Sea* had lost a propeller, the Canadian and American ships were escorted by the Russian icebreaker to the Atlantic, near Spitzbergen. The *Louis S. St. Laurent* has since transited the Northwest Passage on several occasions.

Norman McLeod Rogers. DFO

NORMAN McLEOD ROGERS 1967-1994

Builder:	Canadian Vickers Ltd, Montreal, QC
Date Completed:	1969
Tonnage:	179 (gross)
Dimensions:	295 x 62.5 x 20 (ft) 91 x 19.2 x 6.2 (m)
Machinery:	Twin screw diesel and gas turbine-electric, 12000 SHP (8950 kW)
Speed:	15 kts

(Gas turbines replaced by diesels in 1982)

This ship was designed as a medium powered icebreaker but was also intended to service the large buoys that were replacing lightships. She had the appearance of a very large navigation aids vessel. She was fitted with experimental combined gas turbine and diesel electric machinery. Combined steam and gas (COSAG) and diesel and gas (CODAG) installations were successfully used in several navies, but the Coast Guard did not find them suitable and in 1982 the gas turbines were removed and replaced by diesel engines. In 1990 the ship was transferred to the West Coast, but was soon placed in reserve and in 1994 was sold to Chile for work in the Antarctic. Her name in the Chilean Navy is *Contralmirante Oscar Viel Toro*.

PIERRE RADISSON 1978
FRANKLIN (2)/SIR JOHN FRANKLIN 1979

Builder:	Burrard Drydock Ltd, North Vancouver, BC
Date Completed:	1978 and 1979 respectively

DES GROSEILLIERS 1982

Builder:	Port Weller Drydock, St.Catharines, ON
Date Completed:	1982
Tonnage:	5910 (gross)
Dimensions:	318 x 62 x 23 (ft) 98.1 x 19.1 x 7 (m)
Machinery:	Twin screw diesel-electric, 13600 SHP (10145 kW)
Speed:	16.5 kts

Contrary to the previous Coast Guard practice of building "one off" vessels, usually to the requirements of a particular agency or Region, these three sister ships were built under the Fleet Capital Investment Plan and classed as Medium Gulf/River icebreakers (Type 1200). They were, of course, capable of Arctic operations and were so employed every summer and fall. Although criticized for having two rather than three propellers, they proved to be useful and effective ships.

The *Pierre Radisson* replaced the *N.B. McLean* in the Laurentian Region and the *Franklin*, renamed *Sir John Franklin* in 1980, was an additional ship and was based in Newfoundland.

The *Pierre Radisson* supported shipping in the western Arctic and carried out trials while transiting the Northwest Passage en route to her home port in Quebec. The *Franklin*, attempting to do the same in the following year lost a propeller and had to be rescued by the *Louis S. St. Laurent* and both ships returned via the Panama Canal. The *Des Groseilliers* replaced the *D'Iberville* in the Laurentian Region. All three ships then settled into the routine of icebreaking in the Gulf from January to April and northern deployments from July to October or November. In 1982 the *Pierre Radisson* acted as the Vice-regal yacht when the Governor-

General and Mrs. Schreyer met the heads of state of Denmark, Norway and Iceland in Greenland on the occasion of the 1000th anniversary of the Norse settlement. In October 1997 the *Des Groseilliers,* with a minimal crew and a team of scientists, was left to drift for a full year in the polar ice pack. The mission was to support the US-led international air-sea-ice research project SHEBA (Surface Heat Budget of the Arctic Ocean) The crew and scientists were rotated by a chartered aircraft. These comfortable and successful ships have been the mainstay of the icebreaker fleet.

HENRY LARSEN 1987

Builder:	Versatile Pacific Shipyard Inc., Vancouver, BC
Date Completed:	1987
Tonnage:	6172 (gross)
Dimensions:	323 x 64 x 23 (ft) 99.8 x 19.7 x 7 (m)
Machinery:	Twin screw diesel-electric, 16320 SHP (12175 kW)
Speed:	16.5 kts

The *Henry Larsen* is a modified version of the *Pierre Radisson* class and is also classed as a Type 1200 ship. She has a modified bow with a raised foc'sle, an underwater "ice knife" and an air bubbler system. Instead of six propulsion diesel generators and separate ship service units, the power for all purposes is supplied by three larger units. There is a smaller generator for harbour use, but when the ship is under way, sophisticated electronic controls split the power between the propulsion and domestic loads. On her first voyage, the *Henry Larsen* transited the Northwest Passage to her Maritimes Region base in Dartmouth NS. She was later transferred to the Newfoundland Region.

Polar 8. DFO

THE POLAR 8

(Cancelled in 1990 just before construction was commenced)

Tonnage:	39,000 tonnes (displacement)
Machinery:	Triple screw, diesel or diesel-electric, 107,000 SHP (79820 kW)
Speed:	19 kts

At the time this ship was being designed, the term "Polar" followed by a number was used to indicate the presumed capabilty of a ship in ice. It meant that, in theory, continuous progress could be made through second-year ice that many feet in thickness. It was, of course, an approximation. New ice navigation criteria and classifications have since been developed.

Canadian studies for a Polar icebreaker started in 1971. Designs for a Polar 7 icebreaker were commissioned from several Canadian and foreign companies and received by 1975. Feasibility studies were then undertaken for a nuclear-powered Polar 10, but when a design contract was awarded in 1981 it was for a non-nuclear Polar 8. This was completed and accepted in 1983, but still no construction order was given. In 1987 it was announced that the ship would be built by Versatile Pacific Shipyards, Vancouver, to a design developed by a new consortium; but in February 1990, just before the keel was laid, the project was abruptly canceled.

The ship would have been capable of year-round operation in all Arctic Regions. The reasons for having such a vessel were connected chiefly with Beaufort Sea and other Arctic oil and mineral exploitation forecasts as well as the maintenance of Canadian sovereignty in the area, vis-a-vis the United States. Capable of supporting a large scientific contingent, it would, like the *C.D. Howe,* have carried representatives of several government departments. When Beaufort Sea oil exploration came to an end, and sovereignty concerns diminished, there was no apparent need for such an expensive ship. Milder climatic conditions in later years of the decade appear to show that the decision to cancel the project was correct.

Terry Fox. DFO

TERRY FOX 1991

Builder:	Burrard Yarrows Corp., Vancouver, BC
Date Completed:	1983
Tonnage:	4234 (gross)
Dimensions:	285 x 58 x 27 (ft) 88 x 17.8 x 8.3 (m)
Machinery:	Twin screw controllable pitch diesel, 23200 BHP (17300 kW)
Speed:	16 kts

The *Terry Fox* is one of a group of six outstanding icebreakers built by Gulf OM Ltd, or its subsidiary Canmar, and by Dome Petroleum to support oil exploration and development in the Beaufort Sea. The underwater hull shapes of these ships are very different from conventional Coast Guard icebreakers. They have flat, spoon shaped bows which ride up on the ice and bend it, making it easier to break. With a simpler hull shape, construction time and costs were considerably less than the Type 1200s.

When Beaufort Sea operations slowed in 1987 and came to a halt in 1990, all of these ships, except the *Terry Fox* and her sister the *Kalvik*, were sold foreign. The Coast Guard was able to charter the *Terrry Fox* in 1991 to replace the *John A. Macdonald*. The ship proved satisfactory and economical and was purchased in 1993. The *Kalvik* was operated temporarily by a private Canadian company but was eventually sold as well. Most of these ships now work in the North Sea and in other areas where their icebreaking capability is not needed. Nowadays, the pioneers in icebreaker design are the Finns whose latest government icebreakers are efficient and versatile and will be the pattern for the ships of the future.

CHAPTER 11

THE CABLE SHIP

In 1903, the *Lady Laurier* (Chapter 4) was completed as a combined cable ship and buoy tender. She was intended to service cables to Prince Edward Island and the Gulf of St. Lawrence, but the work was taken over by private interests and her cable facilities were soon removed. Sixty-two years later, another cable ship, the *John Cabot,* was completed. This ship was also designed as an icebreaker and was so employed when not engaged in cable work. As a government vessel, the *John Cabot* was used to maintain cables of a military or classified nature on behalf of the United States Defence Department and the North Atlantic Treaty Organization (NATO).

The *John Cabot* was involved in several dramatic incidents where her special capabilities made the difference between success and failure. In November 1965, in her first year of operation she was called on to repair the cable to the US base at Thule, Greenland. With the ice closing in, and assisted by CCGS *D'Iberville* and USCGC *Westwind,* the repair was accomplished, restoring communication with the Ballistic Early Warning installation at Thule and other vital communication links. In 1973, under the command of Captain Gordon Warren, she successfully rescued the submersible *Pisces III* and its two-man crew from a depth of 480 metres off the coast of Ireland. This complex operation was featured in *Readers Digest* magazine. In 1985, in an operation co-ordinated by Captain Warren from a base at Cork, Ireland, the ship was again the key to success in locating the wreckage and "black boxes" of the Air India Boeing 747 brought down by terrorist bombing in the Atlantic west of Ireland.

With the *John Cabot* as part of the fleet, the Coast Guard was engaged in a technically advanced area of endeavour and its crew had developed considerable expertise. The ship paid for itself with charters to NATO and the US government. However, in the "privatising" climate of the early 90s, it was decided that the ship would be sold to the Crown Corporation, Teleglobe Canada. She passed out of Coast Guard service in 1993 and, not long after, out of Canadian service altogether.

JOHN CABOT 1965-1993

Builder:	Canadian Vickers, Montreal, QC
Date Completed:	1965
Tonnage:	5234 (gross)
Dimensions:	313.2 x 60 x 22 (ft) 96.5 x 18.3 x 6.7 (m)
Machinery:	Twin screw diesel-electric, 9000 SHP (6714 kW)
Speed:	15 kts

The *John Cabot* was the world's only ice-capable cable ship. She operated in the high Arctic and off the coast of Newfoundland, but was usually engaged in servicing marine cables for the United States and NATO. Her equipment was continuously updated and included revolutionary cable burying equipment. In the *Pisces III* rescue operation, she used the US Navy's remotely controlled recovery vehicle, *CURV II*, to hook on to and retrieve the two man submersible *Pisces III* from a depth of 480 metres. In 1985, her own (second generation) cable-burying robotic vehicle, *SCARAB II*, was used to locate and retrieve the wreckage and black boxes from Air India Flight 182 from a depth of 2000 metres. She was sold to Teleglobe Canada in 1993. Two years later she was sold by Teleglobe to a company in the UK and in 2000 was still operating under the Italian flag.

CHAPTER 12
WEATHER SHIPS

Greatly increased air traffic across the Atlantic and Pacific Oceans in the immediate postwar period created a need for accurate weather forecasting. The International Civil Aviation Organization, in conjunction with several governments, including Canada, designated stations in both oceans to be patrolled by weather observation vessels. Even before this, in 1945-46, an RCN corvette, HMCS *Woodstock,* had shared this duty with a United States ship at a station 500 miles westward of Vancouver Island. By 1947 international arrangements had been formalized and from December 1947 to June 1950, the frigate HMCS *St. Stephen* alternated with a USCG ship at Station "Bravo" in the Atlantic.

In 1950 Canada withdrew from the Atlantic station and undertook responsibility for Station "Papa" in the Pacific at Lat. 50°N, Long 145°W. Two frigates: *Stone Town* and *St. Catharines,* were transferred by the RCN to the Department of Transport and were converted at Sorel, Quebec, to specialized weather ships. This included facilities for launching weather balloons and the radar for tracking them. The balloons, as they ascended, transmitted temperature, pressure and humidity data and the radar tracking would provide wind direction and speed. The two ships alternated on the station, starting in December 1950. In 1955, *St. Stephen* was acquired and converted in a similar fashion. She was designated as a spare ship but was seldom needed.

In 1966, two new, purpose-built weather and oceanographic vessels, *Quadra* and *Vancouver,* replaced the frigates. They were fitted with radio beacons which were coded to show in which square of a station grid the ship was located and were in radio contact with transiting aircraft and could provide them with navigation checks and drift data. In addition to their duties as weather ships and navigation aids for aircraft, they provided platforms for oceanographic and fisheries research projects. The ships were available and equipped for search and rescue operations and could act as on-scene co-ordinators. Each ship spent six weeks on station and five weeks in port, with a week taken up by transit time.

In 1974 the *Quadra* operated in the Atlantic in support of the Global Atmospheric Research Program (GARP), a worldwide climatic study conducted by the World Meteorological Organization of the United Nations. During this period she was replaced on station by the hydrographic ship *Parizeau*.

By the early eighties, weather observing satellites, improved electronic navigation systems and faster, higher flying aircraft, made weather ships unnecessary and Station "Papa" was discontinued in 1981.

St. Catharines. DFO

Stone Town. DFO

STONE TOWN 1950-1967

Builder:	Canadian Vickers, Montreal, QC
Date Completed:	1944
Tonnage:	1883 (gross)

ST. CATHARINES 1950-1967
ST. STEPHEN 1955-1967

Builder:	Yarrows Ltd, Esquimalt, BC
Date Completed:	1943 and 1944 respectively
Tonnage:	1895 (gross)

Specifications for all above:

Dimensions:	283 x 36.5 x 13.5 (ft) 86.3 x 11.1 x 4.1 (m)
Machinery:	Twin screw (four cylinder) triple expansion, 5500 IHP
Speed:	18 kts in naval service, but operated at 3700 IHP, c.16 kts as weather ships.

Former RCN frigates. *Stone Town* and *St. Catharines* were converted to weather ships at Sorel, Quebec and entered service on the West Coast in December, 1950. *St. Stephen* was subsequently converted in the same way as her two sisters and in 1955 was stationed on the West Coast as a stand-by vessel and, ultimately, as a source of spares. These frigates were sold in 1967, having being replaced by the purpose-built weather ships, *Quadra* and *Vancouver*.

The first photo (Department of Transport colours) shows *St. Catharines*, the second with Coast Guard insignia is *Stone Town*.

Quadra. DFO

QUADRA (2) 1966-1982
VANCOUVER 1966-1982

Builder:	Burrard Drydock Ltd, North Vancouver, BC
Date Completed:	1966
Tonnage:	5537 (gross)
Dimensions:	414 x 50 x 17.5 (ft) 126.2 x 15.2 x 5.3 (m)
Machinery:	Twin screw steam turbo-electric, 7500 SHP (5595 kW)
Speed:	18 kts

The *Quadra* and *Vancouver* were capacious, comfortable and well equipped ships, but not without drawbacks. Their design had been modified during construction, with additional top weight resulting in a loss of stability. To compensate, some spaces originally intended for fuel had to filled with concrete ballast which meant that, at the end of each period on station, they were low on fuel and could not have responded to a long range search mission. Fortunately this was never put to the test. They were fit-

Vancouver. DFO

ted with a helicopter deck but did not normally carry a helicopter. The conspicuous dome housed radar for tracking aircraft and weather balloons. By 1981, weather ships were no longer considered necessary and *Quadra* and *Vancouver* were retired and sold in 1982.

CHAPTER 13
NAVIGATION AIDS VESSELS

B uoy tenders are the most numerous and general-purpose ships in the Canadian Coast Guard and its predecessors. Their design, usually with a foc'sle and a well deck forward and accommodation aft, became standardized in the early years of the twentieth century. The hold used to stow the buoys was also available for lighthouse supply and for cargo on northern deployments. Twin screws gave manoeuvrability and the later ships were fitted with side thrusters. Larger and medium sized navigation aids vessels were fitted with helicopter decks and hangars. In the nineteen eighties, offshore supply vessel designs were considered for buoy tending and proved to be practical, but the lack of a hold and helicopter facilities limited their use.

As helicopters became a feasible method of supplying lighthouses, or of servicing them after they had been automated, this aspect of the buoy vessels' work diminished; but the new designs were also capable of icebreaking and were increasingly used to keep harbours and the St. Lawrence River open, and to deploy to the Arctic along with the full ice-breakers. The Type 1100 light icebreakers and navigation aids tenders, completed in the eighties, were larger than their predecessors and are able and powerful ships.

This chapter is divided into three parts. In the first group are ships, classed either as light icebreakers or ice-strengthened, of over 1500 tons. The second group is comprised of ice-strengthened ships between 750 and 1500 tons and the third group of small buoy tenders under 750 tons.

First Group. Light icebreakers and ice-strengthened navigation aids tenders over 1500 tons

EDWARD CORNWALLIS (1) 1949-1986

Builder:	Canadian Vickers, Montreal, QC
Date Completed:	1949
Tonnage:	1965 (gross)
Dimensions:	259 x 43.5 x 18 (ft) 79 x 13.3 x 5.5 (m)
Machinery:	Twin screw steam unaflow, 2800 IHP
Speed:	14 kts

This ship was named for the founder of Halifax on the 200th anniversary of that event. The *Cornwallis* was the first postwar ship to be designed and built for the Department of Transport and was the prototype for all the large and medium sized postwar buoy tenders. She was considered as ice-strengthened, rather than a light icebreaker. She was fitted with a helicopter deck in the early 50s and had a hangar added later. Always a popular ship, she was maintained in top condition to the end, with varnished woodwork and shining brass. Briefly renamed *Edward* when awaiting disposal, having been replaced by a new Type 1100 ship with the same name. Decommissioned 1986 and sold 1987.

WALTER E. FOSTER 1954-1985

Builder:	Canadian Vickers, Montreal, QC
Date Completed:	1954
Tonnage:	1672 (gross)
Dimensions:	229 x 42.5 x 160 (ft) 69.9 x 12.9 x 4.9 (m)
Machinery:	Twin screw steam unaflow, 2000 IHP
Speed:	13 kts

An ice-strengthened buoy tender for the Bay of Fundy District, similar to but somewhat smaller than the *Edward Cornwallis*. Fitted with a helicopter deck and hangar. Decommissioned 1985 and sunk as a target by the Navy in 1986.

Montcalm. DFO

Wolfe. DFO

MONTCALM (2) 1957-1987

Builder:	Davie Shipbuilding Ltd, Lauzon, QC
Date Completed:	1957

WOLFE 1959-1986

Builder:	Canadian Vickers Ltd, Montreal, QC
Date Completed:	1959

Specifications for all above

Tonnage:	2017 (gross)
Dimensions:	220 x 48 x 16 (ft) 67 x 14.6 x 4.9 (m)
Machinery:	Twin screw steam unaflow, 4000 IHP
Speed:	13 kts

When completed, these ships were considered to be full icebreakers as they were larger and more powerful than the smaller and older icebreakers, *Saurel* and *Ernest Lapointe*, then in service. Later, however, they were fitted into their proper category of light icebreakers and navigation aids vessels. They were the last of the unaflow engined ships: subsequent light icebreakers were diesel-electric or, in one case, diesel-powered. The *Montcalm* was based in the Laurentian Region. The *Wolfe* changed her homeport on several occasions, from Newfoundland to the Maritimes to the Great Lakes, eventually ending on the West Coast. These ships were built with helicopter decks and had hangars added later. In 1975 the *Wolfe* was fitted with a modified bow to conduct trials which affected the design of later ships. She was sold in 1986. The *Montcalm* was decommissioned in 1987 and broken up at Sydney, NS in 1988.

Sir Humphrey Gilbert. DFO

SIR HUMPHREY GILBERT 1959

Builder:	Davie Shipbuilding Ltd, Lauzon, QC
Date Completed:	1959
Tonnage:	2053 (gross)
Dimensions:	220 x 48 x 16 (ft) 67 x 14.6 x 4 (m)
	After 1986 refit: Length: 238 (ft) 72.5 (m)
Machinery:	Twin screw diesel-electric, 4250 SHP (3170 kW)
Speed:	14 kts

A diesel-electric version of the *Montcalm* and *Wolfe*. The *Sir Humphrey Gilbert* was built with a helicopter deck and had a hangar added later. Stationed in the Newfoundland Region. During her mid-life refit in 1986, she received a modified bow with an air bubbler system (which reduced the hull friction while breaking ice). This lengthened the ship by 18 ft (5.5 m). The second photograph shows the ship after modification.

Sir Humphrey Gilbert. DFO

CAMSELL 1959-1985

Builder: Burrard Drydock Ltd, North Vancouver, BC
Date Completed: 1959
Tonnage: 2022 (gross)
Dimensions: 223.5 x 48 x 16 (ft) 68 x 14.6 x 4.9 (m)
Machinery: Twin screw diesel-electric, 4250 SHP (3170 kW)
Speed: 14 kts

Practically a sister ship to the *Sir Humphrey Gilbert* but different in the appearance of the superstructure. The *Camsell* deployed to the western Arctic each summer. In 1975 and again in 1978 she was badly damaged by ice and her place had to be taken by other ships: by the *J.E.Bernier* in 1976, by the *Narwhal* in 1979 and again by the *J.E.Bernier* in 1980. The *Camsell* was decommissioned in 1985 but not sold until 1989.

SIR WILLIAM ALEXANDER (1)

1959-1990

Builder:	Halifax Shipyard Ltd, Halifax, NS
Date Completed:	1959
Tonnage:	2154 (gross)
Dimensions:	272.5 x 45 x 17.5 (ft) 83 x 13.7 x 5.3 (m)
Machinery:	Twin screw diesel-electric, 4250 SHP (3170 kW)
Speed:	14 kts

This light icebreaker and navigation aids vessel was somewhat longer and narrower than her equivalents in other Regions. She was built with a helicopter deck and the hangar was added later. A successful ship, she was known for rescuing the survivors of the tanker *Kurdistan* that had broken in two in the Cabot Strait in 1977. She was to have been replaced by a Type 1100 ship of the same name in 1987, but as she was still required she continued in service as the *William*. She was sold in 1990.

Alexander Henry. DFO

ALEXANDER HENRY
1959-1986

Builder:	Port Arthur Shipyard, Port Arthur, ON
Date Completed:	1959
Tonnage:	1674 (gross)
Dimensions:	210 x 44 x 16 (ft) 64 x 13.3 x 4.9 (m)
Machinery:	Twin screw diesel, 3550 BHP (2650 kW)
Speed:	13 kts

This ship was stationed in Lake Superior for most of her life. Classed as a light icebreaker but was rather smaller than the other ships in the category and did not have electric propulsion. In 1976 she was used in an interesting experiment in icebreaking with a hover platform pushed in front of the ship (seen in the second photograph). It was not a success, but icebreaking by self-propelled hovercraft is now a proven technique. The *Alexander Henry* became a museum ship at Kingston, Ontario in 1986.

Alexander Henry. DFO

NARWHAL 1963-2000

Builder:	Canadian Vickers, Montreal, QC
Date Completed:	1963
Tonnage:	2064 (gross)
Dimensions:	251.5 x 42 x 12 (ft) 76.7 x 12.8 x 3.7 (m)
Machinery:	Twin screw diesel, 2000 BHP (1490 kW)
Speed:	12 kts
As re-engined:	Twin screw controllable pitch diesel, 3000 BHP (2240 kW)
Speed:	12.5 kts

This ship was designed as an ice-strengthened Arctic depot ship to transport and house stevedores. In this role, she replaced the *Nanook* (Chapter 15) but was also able to act as a navigation aids vessel when not deployed to the north. When private companies took over the bulk of Arctic re-supply, she continued to be employed as a buoy vessel. The *Narwhal* spent some years on the West Coast and deployed to the western Arctic in 1979 to replace the *Camsel,* which had been damaged in ice. She returned

east for a major refit in 1985, which involved extending the flight deck and fitting a hangar. She also received new engines with 50% more power and controllable pitch propellers. Sold in 2000.

J.E. Bernier. DFO

Griffon. DFO

J.E. BERNIER 1967

Builder:	Davie Shipbuilding Ltd, Lauzon, QC
Date Completed:	1967
Tonnage:	2475 (gross)
Dimensions:	231 x 49 x 16 (ft) 70.5 x 14.9 x 4.9 (m)
Machinery:	Twin screw diesel-electric 4250 SHP (3170 kW)
Speed:	13.5 kts

A later version of the group of diesel-electric light ice-breakers and navigation aids tenders. Normally based at Quebec, she twice circumnavigated North America. In 1976 she went through the Panama Canal to replace the damaged *Camsell*, returning through the Northwest Passage after a summer's work in the western Arctic. This assignment was repeated in 1980 and on this occasion, at Cambridge Bay, Victoria Island, she hosted H.E. Governor-General Edward G. Schreyer on the occasion of the 100th anniversary of the transfer of the Arctic archipelago from British to Canadian sovereignty. She was an appropriate choice for this ceremony, as she was named for Captain J.E. Bernier of the CGS *Arctic*, who had provided the official Canadian government presence in the eastern Arctic during the early years of the twentieth century. In 1995 the *J.E. Bernier* was transferred to the Newfoundland Region.

GRIFFON 1970

Builder:	Davie Shipbuilding Ltd, Lauzon, QC
Date Completed:	1970
Tonnage:	2212 (gross)
Dimensions:	234 x 49 x 15.5 (ft) 71.3 x 14.9 x 4.7 (m)
Machinery:	Twin screw diesel-electric 4000 SHP (2985 kW)
Speed:	13.5 kts

The last of the first group of diesel-electric light ice-breakers, she was built for the Central Region and based at Prescott, Ontario. The largest Coast Guard ship permanently stationed in the Great Lakes, but has deployed to Hudson Bay on occasion.

Samuel Risley. DFO

Earl Grey. DFO

SAMUEL RISLEY 1985

Builder:	Vito Construction Ltd, Delta, BC
Date Completed:	1985
Tonnage:	1967 (gross)

EARL GREY (2) 1986

Built:	Pictou Shipyard Ltd, Pictou, NS
Date Completed:	1986
Tonnage:	1988 (gross)

Specifications for all above:

Dimensions:	228.7 x 44.9 x 16.9 (ft) 69.7 x 13.7 x 5.2 (m)
Machinery:	Twin screw controllable pitch diesel, 8640 BHP (6445 kW) (Samuel Risley), 8840 BHP (6595 kW) (Earl Grey)
Speed:	15 kts

In 1980-81 the Type 600 Search and Rescue cutter *Jackman*, a former offshore supply vessel, was fitted with a crane to see if this type of configuration, with the working deck aft, would be suitable for buoy tending. The experiment was a success and in 1983 a contract was place with Robert Allen Ltd, Vancouver, for a navigation aids ship design based on an supply vessel type hull. The two resulting ships were the *Samuel Risley* (named for an early steamship inspector) based in the Central Region and the *Earl Grey*, based in the Maritimes. Under the Fleet Capital Investment Plan system, they are classed as Type 1050.

Geroge R. Pearkes. DFO

Sir Wilfrid Laurier. DFO

MARTHA L. BLACK 1986
GEORGE R. PEARKES 1987

Builder:	Versatile Pacific Shipyard, Vancouver, BC
Date Completed:	1986 and 1987

SIR WILFRID LAURIER 1986

Builder:	Canadian Shipbuilding Ltd, Owen Sound, ON
Date Completed:	1986

ANN HARVEY 1987

Builder:	Halifax Industries Ltd, Halifax, NS
Date Completed:	1987

Specifications for all above:

Tonnage:	3809 to 3823 (gross)
Dimensions:	272.2 x 53.1 x 18.9 (ft) 83 x 16.2 x 5.75 (m)
Machinery:	Twin screw diesel-electric, 7040 SHP (5250 kW)
Speed:	16 kts

A group of light icebreakers and navigation aids vessels classed as Type 1100. They were fitted with an AC/AC electric propulsion system that initially gave some trouble until their sophisticated electronic control system was perfected. At about 3800 tons, they are much larger than the previous group of 2000-ton ships without much increase in buoy or cargo capacity, but are manoeuvrable and are excellent icebreakers. The *Black* and *Pearkes* were built for the Western Region; the *Laurier* for Laurentian Region, and the *Ann Harvey* for Newfoundland service, but the first three have exchanged their stations.

Sir William Alexander. MB Mackay (Private Collection)

EDWARD CORNWALLIS (2) 1986
SIR WILLIAM ALEXANDER (2) 1987

Builder:	Marine Industries Lté, Tracy, QC
Date Completed:	1986 and 1987
Tonnage:	3727 (gross)
Dimensions:	272.2 x 53.1 x 18.9 (ft) 83 x 16.2 x 5.75 (m)
Machinery:	Twin screw diesel-electric, 7040 SHP (5250 kW)
Speed:	16 kts

These Type 1100 ships differ from the other four only by having one less deck to their bridge superstructure, and their buoy handling derricks mounted forward. The *Alexander* had her derricks replaced by a crane in 1998. Both based in the Maritimes.

Edward Cornwallis. DFO

Second Group: Ice strengthened navigation aids tenders, 750–1500 tons

MONTMORENCY 1957-1990

Builder:	Davie Shipbuilding Ltd, Lauzon, QC
Date Completed:	1957
Tonnage:	751 (gross)
Dimensions:	163 x 34 x 11 (ft) 49.7 x 10.2 x 3.4 (m)
Machinery:	Twin screw diesel, 1200 BHP, (932 kW)
Speed:	13 kts

An ice-strengthened navigation aids ship. The *Montmorency* served mostly in the Laurentian Region. Decommissioned 1990, sold (commercial) 1991, but languished in Lunenburg NS for some years until scrapped in 1996.

Tupper. DFO

TUPPER 1959-1999

| Builder: | Marine Industries Ltd, QC |
| Date Completed: | 1959 |

SIMON FRASER 1960

| Builder: | Burrard Drydock Ltd, North Vancouver, BC |
| Date Completed: | 1960 |

Specifications for all above:

Tonnage:	1353 (gross)
Dimensions:	204.5 x 42 x 14 (ft) 62.4 x 12.8 x 4.3 (m)
Machinery:	Twin screw diesel-electric, 2900 SHP (2160 kW)
Speed:	14 kts

Simon Fraser. DFO

These effective ice-strengthened ships were fitted with helicopter decks and hangars. The *Simon Fraser* started her service in the Pacific but in 1986 was converted for Search and Rescue duties in the Laurentian Region. Eventually, she returned to servicing navigation aids in the Maritimes. The *Tupper* was always stationed on the East Coast. She was decommissioned in 1997 and used as an alongside training ship until she was sold to a US owner in 1999. In May 2000 the *Simon Fraser* was loaned to an RCMP support group. She departed Halifax with a volunteer crew, transited via the Panama Canal and arrived in Vancouver six weeks later. On July 1 she sailed to escort the RCMP patrol boat *Nadon,* temporarily re-christened *St. Roch II,* through the Northwest Passage. The mission was to commemorate the *St. Roch's* first transit in 1940-42. The accomplishment of this voyage adds the *Simon Fraser* to the list of Coast Guard vessels to circumnavigate North America.

THOMAS CARLETON (within image) COAST GUARD ✴ GARDE COTIERE

THOMAS CARLETON 1960-1990

Builder:	Saint John Drydock, Saint John, NB
Date Completed:	1960
Tonnage:	1217 (gross)
Dimensions:	204.5 x 42 x 14 (ft) 62.4 x 12.8 x 4.3 (m)
Machinery:	Twin screw diesel, 2000 BHP (1490 kW)
Speed:	13 kts

An ice-strengthened navigation aids vessel for service in the Bay of Fundy, where she spent her entire Coast Guard career. She was decommissioned in 1990 and sold in 1992, when she became the Sea Shepherd organisation's protest ship *Cleveland Amory*. In 1993 she was engaged in a lively joust with Coast Guard and Fisheries and Oceans ships when Paul Watson, Sea Shepherd's founder, attempted to drive Cuban trawlers from the Grand Banks. In the end, she was arrested and was sold for scrap in order to pay the various fines incurred by her owner.

SIMCOE (2) 1962

Builder:	Canadian Vickers, Montreal, QC
Date Completed:	1962

TRACY 1967

Builder:	Port Weller Drydock, St. Catharines, ON
Date Completed:	1967

Specifications for all above:

Tonnage:	962 (gross)
Dimensions:	180 x 38 x 12 (ft) 54.8 x 11.6 x 3.7 (m)
Machinery:	Twin screw diesel-electric, 2000 SHP (1490 kW)
Speed:	14 kts

Ice strengthened navigation aids vessels. *Simcoe* is based at Prescott, Ontario in the Central Region. *Tracy* is based in the Laurentian Region. Handy vessels of an appropriate size for the Great Lakes and the St. Lawrence.

Simcoe. DFO

Tracy. DFO

BARTLETT 1969
PROVO WALLIS 1969

Builder:	Marine Industries Ltd, QC
Date Completed:	1969
Tonnage:	1317 (gross)
Dimensions:	189.3 x 42.5 x 13.2 (ft) 57.7 x 13 x 4.1 (m)
Machinery:	Twin screw controllable pitch diesel, 2100 BHP (1567 kW)
Speed:	12 kts

Provo Wallis as lengthened: 1462 (gross), length 209 (ft) 63.7 (m)

Ice strengthened navigation aids vessels similar in size to the *Tupper* and *Simon Fraser*, but while the earlier ships were graceful and streamlined in appearance these two could only be described as stubby looking and had peculiar large funnels. The *Provo Wallis* was much improved in appearance after being lengthened, in 1990 to 209 ft (63.7 m). The *Bartlett* served in Newfoundland and the Great Lakes, and is currently operated in the Pacific Region, while the *Provo Wallis* has always been employed in the Maritimes.

CP Edwards. Ron Beaupré (Private Collection)

Third Group: Small navigation aids tenders, under 750 tons

C.P. EDWARDS 1946-1972

Builder:	Collingwood Shipbuilding, Collingwood, ON
Date Completed:	1945
Tonnage:	338 (gross)
Dimensions:	144 x 27 x 10 (ft) 44.4 x 8.3 x 3.1 (m)
Machinery:	Single screw triple expansion, 375 IHP
Speed:	10 kts

A small freighter of the "China Coaster" type under construction at the war's end. Taken over in 1946 and converted to a buoy tender and supply vessel in the Parry Sound area. Sold (commercial) 1972.

Alexander MacKenzie. DFO

ALEXANDER MACKENZIE 1950-1988
SIR JAMES DOUGLAS (2) 1956-1996

Builder:	Burrard Drydock, North Vancouver, BC
Date Completed:	1950 and 1956
Tonnage:	576 & 564 (gross)
Dimensions:	150 x 30 x 10 (ft) 45.8 x 9.1 x 3.1 (m)
Machinery:	Twin screw diesel, 1000 BHP (746 kW)
Speed:	12 kts

Useful small navigation aids vessels for the Western Region. Sister ships, but the later vessel was somewhat more rounded in appearance. The *Alexander Mackenzie* was transferred to the Maritimes in 1985, decommissioned in 1988 and sold in 1990. The *Sir James Douglas* was kept in reserve in Victoria during her last years, being activated for short missions when required. Sold in 1996.

Sir James Douglas. DFO

Verendrye. DFO

VERENDRYE 1957-1986

Builder:	Davie Shipbuilding Ltd, Lauzon, QC
Date Completed:	1957
Tonnage:	297 (gross)
Dimensions:	125 x 26 x 7 (ft) 38.1 x 7.9 x 2.1 (m)
Machinery:	Twin screw diesel, 750 BHP (560 kW)
Speed:	11 kts

A small navigation aids vessel stationed in the Great Lakes. Decommissioned 1986. Sold 1988.

Montmagny. DFO

MONTMAGNY (2) 1963-1999

Builder:	Russell Bros. Ltd, Owen Sound, ON
Date Completed:	1963
Tonnage:	328 (gross)
Dimensions:	148 x 29 x 8 (ft) 45.1 x 10.2 x 2.4 (m)
Machinery:	Twin screw diesel, 1000 BHP (746 kW)
Speed:	12 kts

A navigation aids vessel of the smaller class, stationed in the Laurentian Region. Sold 1999.

Kenoki. DFO

Kenoki. DFO

KENOKI 1964-1992

Builder:	Erieau Shipbuilding, ON
Date Completed:	1964
Tonnage:	310 (gross)
Dimensions:	109 x 36 x 6 (ft) 32.9 x 11 x 2.4 (m)
Machinery:	Twin screw diesel, 1000 BHP (746 kW)
Speed:	12 kts

The *Kenoki* was a barge with legs at each corner, which could be lowered to the bottom to steady the vessel when working buoys in fast moving, shallow water. However, in the raised position they affected stability and first one pair and then both were removed in 1973. At the time of this conversion, a new bow was fitted and the two 5-ton pedestal cranes were replaced by a single 10-ton speed crane derrick. The Kenoki was stationed in the Great Lakes. She was decommissioned in 1992 and sold in 1999.

Skidegate. DFO

SKIDEGATE 1964-1988

Builder:	Allied Shipbuilding Ltd, North Vancouver, BC
Date Completed:	1964
Tonnage:	As built 136 (gross)
Dimensions:	87 x 21.5 x 7 (ft) 26.5 x 6.7x 2 (m)
As enlarged:	238 (gross)
Dimensions:	93 x 26.5 x 6.3 (ft) 28.3 x 8 x 1.9 (m)
Machinery:	Twin screw diesel, 320 BHP (240 kW)
Speed:	10 kts

A very small buoy tender that served first on the West Coast and then was transferred to Tuktoyaktuk in the western Arctic. In 1975 she sailed through the Northwest Passage (via Bellot Strait) to Sydney, Nova Scotia, crewed by Coast Guard College staff and cadets. She spent a year as a training ship and was then transferred to the Newfoundland Region. After undergoing a major reconstruction, being enlarged in all dimensions, she was used to maintain navigation aids in Labrador. Sold (commercial) 1988.

Robert Foulis. DFO

ROBERT FOULIS 1969-1999

Builder:	Saint John Drydock, Saint John, NB
Date Completed:	1969
Tonnage:	258 (gross)
Dimensions:	104 x 24 x 7.9 (ft) 31.7 x 7.6 x 2.4 (m)
Machinery:	Twin screw controllable pitch diesel, 960 BHP (715 kW)
Speed:	12 kts

A small buoy tender, based in the Maritimes. She was used as a training ship at the Coast Guard College at Sydney, NS 1994-1996. Sold (commercial) 1999.

Namao. DFO

Tsekoa II. DFO

NAMAO 1975

Builder:	Riverton Boat Works, MB
Date Completed:	1975
Tonnage:	318 (gross)
Dimensions:	110 x 28 x 7 (ft) 33.5 x 8.5 x 2.1 (m)
Machinery:	Twin screw diesel, 1350 BHP (1005 kW)
Speed:	12 kts

Built for service on Lake Winnipeg. In reserve 1998. Reactivated 1999.

TSEKOA II 1995

Built:	North Vancouver, BC
Date Completed:	1984
Tonnage:	161 (gross)
Dimensions:	86.5 x 24.4 x 6.5 (ft) 26.7 x 7.5 x 2.1 (m)
Machinery:	Twin screw diesel, 540 BHP (400 kW)
Speed:	12 kts

Ordered by the Department of Fisheries and Oceans for the Department of Public Works (as DPW could only acquire existing ships). Transferred back to DFO in 1995. The *Tsekoa* was used as a small buoy tender and for search and rescue in the Pacific Region.

COVE ISLE 1980
GULL ISLE 1980

Builder:	Canadian Dredge and Dock Co, Kingston, ON
Date Completed:	1980
Tonnage:	80 (gross)
Dimensions:	65.5 x 19.7 x 5.5 (ft) 20 x 6 x 1.7 (m)
Machinery:	Twin screw controllable pitch diesel 380 BHP (283 kW)
Speed:	11 kts

Previous small buoy tenders under 65 GRT varied in size and material of construction. These small steel buoy tenders were intended for use in restricted and shallow waters and have proven to be very successful. They were followed by four similar but slightly larger craft. These two tenders were employed in the upper St. Lawrence and the Great Lakes.

Cove Isle. DFO

Gull Isle. DFO

Ile des Barques. DFO

Ile Saint-Ours. DFO

PARTRIDGE ISLAND
1985
ILE DES BARQUES
1985
ILE SAINT-OURS
1985
CARIBOU ISLE
1985

Builder:	Breton Industries Ltd, Port Hawkesbury, NS
Date Completed:	1985
Tonnage:	92 (gross)
Dimensions:	75.5 x 19.7 x 5.5 (ft) 23 x 6 x 1.7 (m)
Machinery:	Twin screw controllable pitch diesel, 475 BHP (355 kW)
Speed:	11 kts

A follow-on class to the *Cove Isle* and *Gull Isle*. Lengthened by 10 ft (3 m). The *Ile Saint-Ours* is assigned to the Laurentian Region, the *Ile des Barques* and the *Partridge Island* to the Maritimes Region and the *Caribou Isle* to the Great Lakes. These handy navigation aids tenders, as well as the *Cove Isle* and *Gull Isle*, are classed as Type 800.

CHAPTER 14

SPECIAL RIVER NAVIGATION AIDS TENDERS

The Mackenzie River is a thousand miles long and carries a great amount of water-borne traffic, mostly on barges pushed by special shallow draft tugs designed for the particular conditions found in this enormous but shoal waterway. The navigation season is in the summer and fall: in the winter roads can be built on the frozen surface of the river and its tributaries. To service the navigation aids in the river and on Great Slave Lake, the Coast Guard maintains a base at Hay River on the south side of the lake where, since 1958, specially built navigation aids tenders have been stationed. On the Athabaska, one vessel was based at Fort McMurray until 1998, when improved road links reduced the need for moving goods by water.

In 1974, in anticipation of increased activity generated by oil exploration in the Beaufort Sea, a larger ship, the *Nahidik*, was completed. This vessel continues to work on the Arctic coast of the North West Territories and Victoria Island in conjunction with ships sent annually from Victoria, BC.

The first three buoy tenders were of tug type and usually pushed a barge with a crane to handle the buoys. Later ships, particularly the second *Dumit* and *Eckaloo*, are fully capable and self-contained and are fitted with helicopter decks. Because of the shallow water in which they must operate, they have an unusual propulsion arrangement with their propellers fitted in tunnels. The names of the ships are terms that are associated with navigation or travel in different native languages. Nahidik, for instance, means "pathfinder."

DUMIT (1) 1958-1979
MISKANAW 1958-1997

Builder:	Allied Shipbuilding Ltd, North Vancouver, BC
Date Completed:	1958
Tonnage:	104 (gross)
Dimensions:	64 x 19.7 x 3.9 (ft) 19.5 x 6 x 1.2 (m)
Machinery:	Twin screw diesel, 360 BHP (270 kW)
Speed:	10 kts

Dumit was stationed at Hay River, NWT and operated on the Mackenzie River and Great Slave Lake, while *Miskanaw* maintained the navigation aids on the river and Lake Athabaska. *Dumit* decommissioned in 1979 and was sold (commercial) in 1980. *Miskanaw* became a museum ship at Fort McMurray in 1998.

ECKALOO (1) 1961-1988

Builder:	Allied Shipbuilding Ltd, North Vancouver, BC
Date Completed:	1961
Tonnage:	133 (gross)
Dimensions:	80 x 22 x 4 (ft) 24.4 x 6.7 x 1.2 (m)
Machinery:	Twin screw diesel, 545 BHP (406 kW)
Speed:	11 kts

A slightly enlarged shallow draft buoy vessel for the Mackenzie River system. In 1967 she was lengthened to 115 ft (35 m) and her measurement tonnage increased to 165 (gross). The photo shows her as built. A photo in the colour section shows her after alteration. Sold (commercial) 1988.

TEMBAH 1963

Builder:	Allied Shipbuilding Ltd, North Vancouver, BC
Date Completed:	1963
Tonnage:	189 (gross)
Dimensions:	123 x 26 x 3 (ft) 37.5 x 7.9 x 0.9 (m)
Machinery:	Twin screw diesel, 680 BHP (505 kW)
Speed:	12.5 kts

A further enlargement of the *Eckaloo* design. Like all other vessels of this type, except the *Miskanaw,* she was based at Hay River on the Great Slave Lake. The photograph shows how shallow is the draft of these special vessels. Since 1998, the *Tembah* has been maintained in reserve to replace the *Eckaloo* (2) if conditions warrant. The *Tembah's* draft is only 3 ft (0.9 m) compared to the *Eckaloo's* (5.2 ft or 1.4 m).

NAHIDIK 1974

Builder:	Allied Shipbuilding Ltd, North Vancouver, BC
Date Completed:	1974
Tonnage:	856 (gross)
Dimensions:	175.2 x 49.9 x 6.6 (ft) 53.3 x 15.2 x 2 (m)
Machinery:	Twin screw diesel, 4300 BHP (3205 kW)
Speed:	14 kts

A much larger, ice-strengthened, shallow draft vessel for servicing navigation aids, re-supply and general duties in the Mackenzie River delta and along the Arctic coast. Fitted with a helicopter deck.

DUMIT (2) 1979

Builder:	Allied Shipbuilding Ltd, North Vancouver, BC
Date Completed:	1979
Tonnage:	569 (gross)
Dimensions:	160.8 x 40 x 5.2 (ft) 49 x 12.2 x 1.6 (m)
Machinery:	Twin screw diesel, 2250 BHP (1680 kW)
Speed:	13.5 kts

A larger and more capable shallow draft buoy tender, fitted with a helicopter deck. Based at Hay River and employed on Great Slave Lake and the Mackenzie River, replacing the older ship of the same name.

Eckaloo. DFO

ECKALOO (2) 1988

Builder:	Vancouver Shipyard Ltd, Vancouver, BC
Date Completed:	1988
Tonnage:	661 (gross)
Dimensions:	160.8 x 44 x 5.2 (ft) 49 x 13.4 x 1.4 m)
Machinery:	Twin screw diesel, 2120 BHP (1580 kW)
Speed:	12.5 kts

A near sister to the *Dumit (2)* but with steel, instead of aluminium, upper works, necessitating an increase in beam to maintain stability. Fitted with a helicopter deck. She replaced the older ship of the same name.

CHAPTER 15

NORTHERN SUPPLY VESSELS

T he assumption by Canada of the responsibility for delivering most of the cargo to DEW line and other defence sites led to the acquisition of nine shallow draft former landing craft. While not ice-strengthened, they could be escorted by ice-breakers, were economical to operate and were designed to take the ground. As the tidal range in the eastern Arctic is large, they could come inshore at high water and when the tide receded the cargo would be unloaded into trucks. This method is still used by barges and freighters.

The landing craft were at first given numbers, but later the names shown here were assigned. These vessels were sold after commercial ships took over the re-supply work, except for deliveries to the most northern and most ice-bound destinations, which are handled by Coast Guard icebreakers.

MINK 1958-1975/76

Built:	Chepstow, UK

MARMOT 1958-1975/76

Built:	Belfast, UK
Date Completed:	1944

Specifications for all above:

Tonnage:	543 (gross)
Dimensions:	187 x 34 x 4 (ft) 57 x 10.3 x 1.2 (m)
Machinery:	Twin screw diesel, 920 BHP (686 kW)
Speed:	9 kts

The *Mink* and *Marmot* were British landing craft of the LCT 4 type. They were little modified and were used in the Arctic principally as lighters, bringing cargo from large ships inshore, where it could be unloaded at low tide, as shown in the second

Marmot. DFO

photograph. They were sold when commercial interests took over the work of northern re-supply.

AUK   EIDER
GANNET   PUFFIN   1957/61-1971/82
RAVEN   SKUA

Builder:	Sir Wm. Arrol, Glasgow, Scotland (*Auk, Eider, Gannet, Skua*)
Builder:	Harland and Wolff, Belfast (*Puffin* and *Raven*)

Specifications for all above:

Tonnage:	1089 (gross)
Dimensions:	231 x 38 x 7 (ft) 70.5 x 11.6 x 2.1 (m)
Machinery:	Twin screw diesel, 1000 BHP (746 kW)
Speed:	8 kts

Raven. DFO

These vessels were former British landing craft of the larger LCT 8 type, completed just postwar. They were considerably modified, some with new bows (no bow doors) and cranes or derricks added. Some were given cargo fuel tanks. They were used for northern re-supply and some were occasionally employed as buoy vessels. *Auk* and *Gannet* were sold in 1971, *Raven* in 1973, *Puffin* in 1979, *Skua* in 1981 and *Eider* in 1982. The mast and derrick arrangements varied. The first photo shows the *Gannet*. She still has the bow door, probably welded shut. The second is the *Raven* with different masting and a new conventional bow.

NANOOK 1960-1965

Builder:	Sir Wm. Arrol, Glasgow, Scotland
Date Completed:	1946
Tonnage:	1155 (gross)
Dimensions:	220 x 38 x 7 (ft) 70.5 x 11.6 x 2.1 (m)
Machinery:	Twin screw diesel, 1320 BHP (985 kW)
Speed:	9 kts

The *Nanook* was an LCT 8 type modified as a depot and accommodation vessel for the stevedores that unloaded ships and the other landing craft in the Arctic. She had a short life: in 1963 she was badly damaged in ice and, on returning to Halifax, was placed in reserve until 1965, when she was sold. She was replaced as a depot ship by the *Narwhal* (see Chapter 13).

CHAPTER 16

SEARCH AND RESCUE CUTTERS

When the Coast Guard was formally constituted in February 1962, the only dedicated rescue units in the existing fleet were a handful of locally manned, diesel-powered lifeboats in the 32-35 ft range, the latest of which had been built in 1951. Of course, all government ships were used in the rescue role when needed and by the custom of the sea, all ships are obliged to respond to a distress call if they are capable of doing so.

Measures to improve the search and rescue (SAR) capability soon initiated. Two fast Air Sea Rescue boats were transferred from the RCAF and new types of rescue vessel were ordered and, within a few years, were added to the fleet. Six 95 ft cutters of similar type to those used by the United States Coast Guard, along with three 70 ft boats went into service in 1963 and 1964 (one of the larger type was temporarily assigned to fisheries patrol duties). In 1967 the first of eighteen self-righting lifeboats of USCG design was on station at Clark's Harbour, Nova Scotia, and in 1969 the large and fast offshore patrol cutter *Alert* was completed by Davies Shipyard at Lauzon, Quebec. This ship was originally considered to be the prototype for a whole class of large cutters, but no more were built. Instead, a former RCMP vessel, the *Wood*, renamed *Daring*, was acquired as a running mate.

In 1977 an offshore supply vessel, the *Cathy B,* was chartered for SAR duties in Newfoundland and proved so successful she was purchased along with two sister ships. Later, two more of the type were acquired while still under construction. In the 80s, a pair of small ice-strengthened vessels of fishing boat type were provided to aid inshore fishing vessels on the northern Newfoundland coast, while two intermediate type cutters were built to replace the remaining 95 ft vessels.

Starting in 1989, eleven 52 ft self-righting lifeboats of UK design were acquired or built. As they were faster and had a longer range, each replaced two 44 footers. It appears that the Coast Guard is now reverting to US designs, with a new 47 ft type, similar to those in the USCG. In sheltered waters, fast planing-hull utility boats and rigid hull inflatable craft provide rescue services. Some stations are crewed by temporary employees, often students, during the summer months. Another element of the search and rescue organization is the Coast Guard Auxiliary of capable fishing vessels and yachts, which are often the first to respond to a local emergency. On the West Coast, hovercraft, (See Chapter 23), have provided search and rescue services since 1968.

Racer. DFO

RALLY 1963-1983

Builder: Davie Shipbuilding Ltd, Lauzon, QC

RAPID 1963-1983

Builder: Ferguson Industries, Pictou, NS

RELAY 1963-1989

Builder: Kingston Shipbuilding, Kingston, ON

READY 1963-1991

Builder: Burrard Drydock, Vancouver, BC

RACER 1963-1991
RIDER 1969-1987

Builder: Yarrows Ltd, Victoria, BC

Specifications for all above:

Date Completed:	1963
Tonnage:	140 (gross)
Dimensions:	95.2 x 19.7 x 6.2 (ft) 29 x 6 x 1.9 (m)
Machinery:	Twin screw diesel, 2400 BHP (1790 kW)
Speed:	15 kts

Six search and rescue cutters by various builders, based on a United States Coast Guard design. Three were based in the Maritimes, one deploying to the Great Lakes every summer, and three in the Pacific. *Rider* was initially named *Hunter Point* and employed as a fisheries patrol vessel, but was returned to the Coast Guard in 1969. The value of these cutters was immediately apparent and they participated in many rescues on both coasts. *Rally* and *Rapid* were transferred to the Navy in 1983 for use as training vessels for the Naval Reserve. *Rider* was sold in 1987. *Relay* became a museum ship at Haute-Richelieu in 1989. *Ready* and *Racer* were decommissioned in 1991 and sold in 1992.

Alert. DFO

Alert. DFO

ALERT (2) 1969-1997

Builder:	Davie Shipbuilding Ltd, Lauzon, QC
Date Completed:	1969
Tonnage:	1752 (gross)
Dimensions:	234.3 x 39.7 x 16.1 (ft) 71.4 x 12.1 x 4.9 (m)
Machinery:	Twin screw controllable pitch diesel, 7874 BHP (5875 kW)
Speed:	18 kts

A large offshore search and rescue cutter with a helicopter deck and hangar. The *Alert* was always based in the Maritimes. Although she was given a life extension refit in 1987, she was placed in reserve in 1994. In 1995 and 1996 she was laid up at the Bedford Institute of Oceanography and temporarily used by Fisheries and Oceans as a patrol vessel and by the Navy as a train-ing ship, but neither department wanted her permanently. The *Alert* was sold to commercial interests in 1997 and renamed *Ocean Alert*.

Daring. DFO

DARING 1971-1986

Builder:	Davie Shipbuilding Ltd, Lauzon, QC
Date Completed:	1958
Tonnage:	657 (gross)
Dimensions:	231 x 38 x 7 (ft) 70.5 x 11.6 x 2.1 (m)
Machinery:	Twin screw diesel, 2660 BHP (1985 kW)
Speed:	16 kts

Daring was built for the RCMP as the patrol vessel *Wood*. She was transferred to the Coast Guard in 1971 and partnered the *Alert* on offshore search and rescue patrols in the Maritimes. She was replaced by the *Mary Hichens* and sold in 1986. This ex RCMP, ex Coast Guard vessel was later arrested in Belize in Central America as a drug running mother ship.

George E. Darby. DFO

GEORGE E. DARBY 1977-1992

Builder:	Bel-Aire Shipyard, Vancouver, BC
Date Completed:	1972
Tonnage:	942 (gross)
Dimensions:	174.6 x 45.1 x 13.3 (ft) 56.1 x 13.7 x 4 (m)
Machinery:	Twin screw controllable pitch diesel, 3940 BHP (2940 kW)
Speed:	13.5 kts

An offshore supply vessel, built as the *Janie B.* and soon renamed *Cathy B.* With the success of the *Alert* and *Daring* in the Maritimes, the Newfoundland Region chartered the *Cathy B.* in 1977 to assess the suitability of this type of vessel for Coast Guard use. As a result of a year's experience, two more supply ships were purchased for Newfoundland, and the *Cathy B* was also purchased, renamed *George E. Darby*, and sent to the Pacific. All these ships were modified by extending the deckhouse to add a hospital area and additional accommodation. Sold in 1992.

Grenfell. DFO

GRENFELL 1978-1990
JACKMAN 1979-1992

Builder:	Bel-Aire Shipyard, Vancouver, BC
Date Completed:	1972
Tonnage:	877 (gross)
Dimensions:	174.6 x 45.1 x 13.3 (ft) 56.1 x 13.7 x 4 (m)
Machinery:	Twin screw controllable pitch diesel, 4890 BHP (3650 kW)
Speed:	14 kts

Offshore supply vessels, formerly *Baffin Service* and *Hudson Service*. Purchased 1978 and 1979 and modified for Coast Guard search and rescue service in the Newfoundland Region. Sold (commercial) in 1990 and 1992.

MARY HICHENS 1985-2000

Builder:	Marystown Shipyard Ltd, NFLD
Date Completed:	1985
Tonnage:	1684 (gross)
Dimensions:	210.6 x 45 x 15.6 (ft) 64 x 13.7 x 4.7 (m)
Machinery:	Twin screw controllable pitch diesel, 7420 BHP (5535 kW)
Speed:	15 kts

An offshore supply vessel, originally to be named *Beau Bois*, taken over by the Coast Guard while under construction and converted to a search and rescue cutter. The *Mary Hichens* was an ice-strengthened ship. She replaced the *Daring* in the Maritimes Region. In 2000 she was sold to commercial interests for service in East Asia.

Mary Hichens. DFO

Sir Wilfred Grenfell. DFO

SIR WILFRED GRENFELL

1987

Builder:	Marystown Shipyard Ltd, NFLD
Date Completed:	1987
Tonnage:	2403 (gross)
Dimensions:	224.7 x 49.2 x 16.4 (ft) 68.5 x 15 x 5 (m)
Machinery:	Twin screw controllable pitch diesel, 12180 BHP (9085 kW)
Speed:	16 kts

A very powerful, ice-strengthened offshore supply vessel. Like the *Mary Hichens,* she was taken over by the Coast Guard while under construction and converted to a search and rescue cutter. All these ships and the *Alert* were classed as Type 600 vessels.

Gordon Reid. DFO

GORDON REID 1990
JOHN JACOBSON 1990-2001

Builder:	Versatile Pacific Shipyard, Vancouver, BC
Date Completed:	1990
Tonnage:	836 (gross)
Dimensions:	164 x 36 x 17 (ft) 50 x 11 x 5.2 (m)
Machinery:	Twin screw diesel, 3480 BHP (2670 kW)
Speed:	16 kts

Intermediate search and rescue cutters, classed as Type 500 vessels. They replaced the "R" class cutters in BC waters and were larger and far more capable vessels than their predecessors. The *John Jacobson* was laid up in 1999 and sold in 2001 to the Université du Québec in Rimouski for conversion to a research vessel.

Harp. DFO

HARP 1986
HOOD 1986

Builder:	Georgetown Shipyard, PEI
Date Completed:	1986
Tonnage:	179 (gross)
Dimensions:	80.4 x 27.6 x 7.9 (ft) 24.5 x 8.5 x 2.4 (m)
Machinery:	Twin screw controllable pitch diesel, 850 BHP (635 kW)
Speed:	10 kts

Small ice-strengthened cutters of fishing vessel type for use in northern Newfoundland waters. Classed as Type 200.

Spindrift. DFO

Cape Hurd. DFO

Small search and rescue cutters, classed as Type 400

Three, built of wood with double diagonal planking: *Spindrift, Spray* and *Spume* were all stationed in the Great Lakes (1964 to 1992). They were 70 ft (23 m) long and designed for 19 kts.

Four similar steel vessels, *Isle Rouge, Point Henry, Point Race* and *Cape Hurd* were built in 1980-82, one for the Laurentian Region, one for the Great Lakes and two for the Pacific.

Westfort. DFO

Cape Sutil. DFO

Cap-aux-Meules. DFO

Bittern. DFO

Self-righting lifeboats, classed as Type 300

CG 101, a standard United States Coast Guard 44 ft self right-ing lifeboat built at the USCG yard, Curtis, Maryland, was acquired in 1967. Seventeen others were built in Canada by var-ious shipyards between 1969 and 1985. They were stationed in areas of dense inshore traffic and were relied on by fishermen and pleasure boaters in all coastal areas. These boats were not regis-tered vessels and numbering was not consistent. They were known by the geographical name of their station.

In 1989 a larger 52 ft (15.8 m) fibreglass lifeboat of the British "Arun" type was purchased from Halmatic, Havant, England and named *Bickerton*, for its station in Nova Scotia. Ten others were built in Canada of aluminium, some taking station names and others reviving the Type 400 "S" names, while the Newfoundland boats were the *W. Jackman* and *W.G. George*.

In 1998 the *Cape Sutil*, a 47 ft boat of the latest USCG type, was built at Kingston, ON. Two more, *Cape Calvert* and *Cape St. James* were delivered in 1999, two in 2000 and two in 2001, all with Cape names.

A variety of fast utility craft, designated Type 100, are sta-tioned in more sheltered waters.

CHAPTER 17

THE RCMP MARINE DIVISION

None of the major vessels that had been incorporated into the Royal Canadian Navy in 1939 were returned to the RCMP at the end of the war in 1945. Two, *Macdonald* and *Laurier,* became fisheries patrol vessels and the rest were sold. A new fleet of former naval vessels was acquired and the pre-war arrangements with the RCN with respect to bases, stores, refits and training were renewed. The major elements of the new fleet were three Bangor class minesweepers, known in the RCMP as the Commissioner class, and two Fairmile motor launches, as well as smaller craft. In April 1947 the Marine Section became the Marine Division with headquarters in Halifax. Unlike the pre-war ship's companies, the Marine personnel wore regular RCMP uniforms and were full members of the Force with respect to pay, pension and privileges.

In 1952, a ten-year construction program was contemplated but only two of the larger class of vessel were actually completed—*Wood* in 1958 as a replacement for the Commissioner class and *Fort Steele* to replace the Fairmiles. Smaller patrol boats, outside the scope of this book, were also added to the fleet. However, in 1970, the Marine Division was discontinued. The larger vessels were soon transferred to other departments while the various regional divisions took over the smaller craft and the responsibility for providing marine services. In the last decade the inshore craft crewed by the Force have grown in size. The Force now operates five fast catamaran patrol vessels of the larger type (17-20 metres). *Nadon, Higgitt, Lindsay* and the slightly larger *Inkster* are stationed on the West Coast and *Simmonds* on the south coast of Newfoundland. In 2000 the *Nadon,* temporarily renamed *St. Roch II,* transited the Northwest Passage escorted by the *Simon Fraser,* to commemorate Henry Larsen's exploits during the Second World War (see Chapter 2).

French. NAC PA209437

FRENCH (2) 1945-1960
MACBRIEN 1945-1960
IRVINE 1945-1962

Builder:	Davie Shipbuilding Ltd, Lauzon, QC
Date Completed:	1941
Tonnage:	581 (gross)
Dimensions:	155.4 x 27.9 x 14.6 (ft) 47.4 x 8.5 x 4.5 (m)
Machinery:	Twin screw diesel, 2000 BHP, (1490 kW)
Speed:	16 kts

Bangor class minesweepers, transferred from the RCN at the end of the Second World War and known as the Commissioner class. *French* was formerly HMCS *Transcona*, *MacBrien* ex HMCS *Trois Rivières* and *Irvine* ex HMCS *Noranda*. Several others were assigned to the RCMP but not, in the end, handed over. *French* and *MacBrien* were sold for scrap in 1960 and *Irvine* was sold in 1962 for conversion to a yacht.

MacBrien. RCMP HQ

Fort Walsh. RCMP Museum of Regina

FORT WALSH 1945-1959
FORT PITT 1945-1959

Built:	various builders during WW2
Tonnage:	65 tons displacement
Dimensions:	112 x 17.8 x 5 (ft) 34.5 x 5.4 x 1.5 (m)
Machinery:	Twin screw diesel, 1260 BHP (940 kW)
Speed:	20 kts

Former Fairmile type motor launches transferred from the RCN. Two others, *Fort Selkirk* and *Fort Steel* (sic), do not appear to have been put into service. Both sold in 1959.

Fort Steele. RCMP Museum of Regina

FORT STEELE 1955-1973

Builder:	Canadian Shipbuilding & Engineering Co
Date Completed:	1955
Tonnage:	85 tons (displacement)
Dimensions:	118 x 21 x 7 (ft) 36 x 6.4 x 2.1 (m)
Machinery:	Twin screw diesel, 2800 BHP (2088 kW)
Speed:	20 kts

A steel and aluminium fast patrol craft stationed in the Atlantic. When the RCMP marine section was reduced to small inshore craft, *Fort Steele* was transferred to the Navy and commissioned in 1973 as a training ship for Naval Reserves.

VICTORIA 1955-1976

Builder: Yarrows Ltd, Victoria, BC
Date Completed: 1955

BLUE HERON 1956-1968

Builder: Hunter Boat Works, Orillia, ON
Date Completed: 1956

Specifications for all above:

Tonnage:	66 tons displacement
Dimensions:	92 x 17 x 5.5 (ft) 28 x 5.2 x 1.7 (m)
Machinery:	twin screw diesel, 1200 BHP (895 kW)
Speed:	14 kts

Of similar design, *Victoria* was built of steel but *Blue Heron* was a "Bird" class naval patrol craft transferred from the RCN just after completion, and was built of wood. She was returned to the RCN in 1968.

Wood. RCMP Museum of Regina

WOOD 1958-1971

Builder:	Davie Shipbuilding Ltd, Lauzon, QC
Date Completed:	1958
Tonnage:	657 (gross)
Dimensions:	231 x 38 x 7 (ft) 70.5 x 11.6 x 2.1 (m)
Machinery:	Twin screw diesel, 2660 BHP (1985 kW)
Speed:	16 kts

This ship was transferred to the Coast Guard as an offshore search and rescue cutter in 1971. Renamed *Daring*. (See Chapter 16)

217   THE RCMP MARINE DIVISION

NADON, HIGGETT, LINDSAY

Builder: Shore Boatbuilders, Richmond, BC
Date Completed: 1991, 1992 and 1993

SIMMONDS

Builder: Chantier Navale, Matane, QC
Date Completed: 1995

Specifications for all above:

Dimensions: 57.75 x 22 x 1.87 (ft) 17.6 x 6.7 x 0.67 (m)
Machinery: Twin screw diesel, 1640 BHP (1223 kW)
Speed: Cruising speed 25 kts, Maximum 35 kts

Fast aluminum catamaran patrol craft. In 2000 *Nadon* was temporarily renamed *St. Roch II* and transited the Northwest Passage to commemorate the historic wartime voyage of the original *St. Roch. Simmonds* is stationed in Newfoundland, the others in British Columbia.

INKSTER

Builder: Allied Shipbuilders Ltd, North Vancouver, BC
Date Completed: 1996
Dimensions: 64.75 x 22 x 1.87 (ft) 19.7 x 6.7 x 0.67 (m)

Of similar design but longer than the *Nadon* type. Stationed in northern British Columbia.

CHAPTER 18

FISHERIES PATROL VESSELS

The old trawlers that had been used for offshore fisheries patrol between the wars had all been requisitioned by the RCN in 1939 and by 1945 were worn out. To replace them, a minesweeper was converted for offshore fisheries patrol on the East Coast, while on the West Coast a pair of former RCMP patrol craft, that had also served with the RCN during the war, were employed on coastal fisheries duties. It was not until 1959 that the first of the new construction postwar fisheries patrol vessels joined the fleet. Her general design was similar to that of the old *Malaspina* and *Galiano* (see Chapter 5). Like the Bangor class ship she replaced on the East Coast, she was christened *Cygnus*.

In the sixties and seventies the responsibilities of the fisheries patrol service were greatly enlarged. On 16 July 1964, Canada expanded its territorial sea limits from three miles to twelve. On 1 January 1977, a two-hundred-mile exclusive economic zone was proclaimed, applicable both for mineral exploration and development and for the fisheries. From this time on, foreign vessels fished within the zone only by permission. Canadian vessels were also regulated. To patrol the enlarged area, three new offshore vessels were added to the fleet (*Cape Freels* type). These were followed by two improved versions in the seventies, which included yet another *Cygnus*. A group of smaller aluminium hulled coastal craft also joined the service. They did not prove entirely satisfactory and one was converted to a research vessel.

The majority of the vessels supporting fisheries conservation and protection are small craft, similar to the inshore fishing vessels that they police. They are stationed in the areas of maximum coastal fishing activity and have crews of three or five, usually local people with an intimate knowledge of their area of responsibility. Some examples of these smaller craft are illustrated in this chapter.

CYGNUS (1) 1946-1959

Builder:	Davie Shipbuilding Ltd, Lauzon, QC
Date Completed:	1941
Tonnage:	581 (gross)
Dimensions:	155.4 x 27.9 x 14.6 (ft) 47.4 x 8.5 x 4.5 (m)
Machinery:	Twin screw diesel, 2000 BHP (1490 kW)
Speed:	16 kts

A Bangor class minesweeper. As HMCS *Melville,* she served in the RCN until 1945. In 1946 she became the fisheries protection vessel *Cygnus* and was stationed on the East Coast. She was retired in 1959 and replaced by *Cygnus (2).* Broken up in 1961.

Laurier. DFO

HOWAY 1946-1982
LAURIER 1946-1984

Builder:	Morton Engineering & Drydock Ltd, Quebec City, QC
Date Completed:	1936
Tonnage:	201 (gross)
Dimensions:	113 x 21 x 10.3 (ft) 34.5 x 6.4 x 3.1 (m)
Machinery:	(re-engined) Twin screw diesel, 1000 BHP
Speed:	13 kts

The former RCMP vessels *Macdonald* and *Laurier*. Both ships had served in the RCN from 1939 to 1945. In 1946 they were transferred to the Fisheries Department and based in British Columbia. The *Macdonald* was renamed *Howay* but *Laurier* retained her original name. Sold 1982 and 1984.

CYGNUS (2) 1959-1981

Builder:	Canadian Vickers, Montreal, QC
Date Completed:	1959
Tonnage:	524 (gross)
Dimensions:	153 x 28 x 10 (ft) 46.6 x 8.5 x 3 (m)
Machinery:	Single screw diesel, 1000 BHP (746 kW)
Speed:	14 kts
Re-engined 1969:	1600 BHP (5250 kW)
Speed:	14.5 kts

The first postwar purpose-built offshore fisheries patrol vessel. She replaced *Cygnus (1)* and was based in the Maritimes. Her machinery layout of two diesels geared to a single shaft was to be repeated in later vessels. She was retired in 1981 and renamed *Lamna* to free her name for the new fisheries patrol vessel *Cygnus (3)*. Sold for conversion to a seismic research vessel (*Arctic Prowler*) in 1983.

HUNTER POINT 1963-1969

Builder:	Yarrows Ltd, Victoria, BC
Date Completed:	1963
Tonnage:	140 (gross)
Dimensions:	95.2 x 19.7 x 6.2 (ft) 29 x 6 x 1.9 (m)
Machinery:	Twin screw diesel, 2400 BHP (1790 kW)
Speed:	15 kts

An "R" class search and rescue cutter (see Chapter 16). Employed as a fisheries patrol vessel on the West Coast until 1969, when she was transferred to the Coast Guard as an extra SAR cutter and renamed *Rider*.

(See Chapter 16 for photo.)

Cape Freels. DFO

Chebucto. DFO

CAPE FREELS 1962-1976

Builder:	Halifax Shipyard, Halifax, NS
Date Completed:	1962

CHEBUCTO 1966-1998

Builder:	Ferguson Industries Ltd, Pictou, NS
Date Completed:	1966

Specifications for all above:

Tonnage:	750 (gross)
Dimensions:	179 x 30.8 x 12.1 (ft) 54.6 x 9.4 x 3.7 (m)
Machinery:	Single screw controllable pitch diesel. 2520 BHP (1882 kW)
Speed:	13 kts

Steel offshore fisheries patrol vessels and enlarged versions of the *Cygnus (2)*. *Cape Freels* was stationed in the Newfoundland Region. In March 1976, she caught fire while on patrol and had to be abandoned. The 23 crew members spent 15 hours in a liferaft before being rescued. The ship subsequently sank while in tow of CCGS *John Cabot*. *Chebucto* was stationed in the Maritimes Region and sold in 1998.

Tanu. DFO

TANU 1968

Builder:	Yarrows Ltd, Esquimalt, BC
Date Completed:	1968
Tonnage:	754 (gross)
Dimensions:	164.3 x 32 x 15.6 (ft) 50.1 x 9.75 x 4.75 (m)
Machinery:	Single screw controllable pitch diesel: 2640 BHP (1968 kW)
Speed:	14 kts

A fisheries patrol vessel similar in size and concept to the *Cape Freels* and *Chebucto* but differing in appearance. The *Tanu* was considered to be superior in finish to her near sisters. Employed on patrols in the Pacific.

Cape Roger. DFO

Cygnus. DFO

CAPE ROGER 1977

Builder: Ferguson Industries Ltd, Pictou, NS
Date Completed: 1977

CYGNUS (3) 1982

Builder: Marystown Shipyard Ltd, NFLD
Date Completed: 1982

Specifications for all:

Tonnage:	1255 & 1210 (gross)
Dimensions:	205 x 35.5 x 12.5 (ft) 62.5 x 10.8 x 3.8 (m)
Machinery:	Single screw controllable pitch diesel, 4395 BHP (3278 kW)
Speed:	17 kts

These improved and enlarged developments of the *Chebucto* are successful offshore fisheries patrol vessels. *Cape Roger* is stationed in the Newfoundland Region and *Cygnus* in the Maritimes. Both have helicopter decks but only *Cape Roger* has a hangar.

Cape Harrison. DFO

CAPE HARRISON 1976-1983
LOUISBOURG 1977

Builder:	Breton Industries Ltd, Port Hawkesbury, NS
Date Completed:	1976 and 1977
Tonnage:	295 (gross)
Dimensions:	124 x 27 x 6.9 (ft) 37.8 x 8.2 x 2.6 (m)
Machinery:	Twin screw diesel. 4500 BHP (3310 kW)
Speed:	18 kts (never attained)
As re-engined:	2400 BHP (1790 kW)
Speed:	13.5 kts

Aluminium coastal fisheries patrol vessels. In 1983 *Cape Harrison* was converted for oceanographic research and renamed *Louis M. Lauzier* (see Chapter 19). *Louisbourg* continued to be employed on East Coast fisheries patrols. The *Louisbourg* was

Louisbourg. DFO

originally based in Halifax and employed on fisheries patrols in the Gulf of St. Lawrence. She was transferred to the Laurentian Region in 1993.

James Sinclair. DFO

Leonard J. Cowley. DFO

Leonard J. Cowley. DFO

JAMES SINCLAIR

1981-1998

Builder:	J. Manly Ltd, New Westminster, BC
Date Completed:	1981
Tonnage:	298 (gross)
Dimensions:	124 x 27 x 6.9 (ft) 37.8 x 8.2 x 2.6 (m)
Machinery:	Twin screw diesel, 2400 BHP (1790 kW)
Speed:	13.5 kts

An aluminium coastal fisheries patrol vessel similar to *Cape Harrison* and *Louisbourg*. Employed on West Coast fisheries patrols. Retired 1998. Sold 2000.

LEONARD J. COWLEY

1984

Builder:	West Coast Manly Shipyard Ltd, Vancouver, BC
Date Completed:	1984
Tonnage:	2243 (gross)
Dimensions:	236 x 46.5 x 14.8 (ft) 72 x 14.2 x 4.5 (m)
Machinery:	Single screw controllable pitch diesel. 4235 BHP (3160 kW)
Speed:	15 kts

An ice-strengthened, offshore fisheries patrol vessel, fitted with a helicopter deck and hangar. Near sister to the hydrographic / oceanographic research ship *John P. Tully*. The *Cowley* is stationed in the Newfoundland Region.

LE QUEBECOIS 1987

Builder:	Chantier Maritimes, Paspebiac, QC
Date Completed:	1968
Tonnage:	186 (gross)
Dimensions:	93 x 23 x 10 (ft) 28.3 x 7.1 x 3.1 (m)
Machinery:	Single screw controllable pitch diesel 510 BHP (380 kW)
Speed:	11 kts

Built as a training vessel for the École de pêche, provinciale du Québec. Purchased by DFO in 1987 and used as a fisheries patrol vessel.

The photo shows her just after being repainted in Coast Guard colours.

Arrow Post. DFO

ARROW POST 1991

Builder:	Hike Metal Products, Wheatley, ON
Date Completed:	1991
Tonnage:	228 (gross)
Dimensions:	89.5 x 39.4 x 11 (ft) 27.3 x 12 x 3.4 (m)
Machinery:	Single screw controllable pitch diesel, 1280 BHP (954 kW)
Speed:	13 kts

A steel coastal fisheries patrol vessel, stationed in the Pacific. Note: "Post" names are usually given to smaller inshore fisheries patrol vessels.

Bonilla Rock. DFO

Typical inshore patrol vessels

These craft are 12-15 metres long, built of wood or fibreglass.

CHAPTER 19

FISHERIES RESEARCH VESSELS

In 1937, the Fisheries Research Board was established to conduct research into practical and economic problems connected with marine and freshwater fisheries. In the postwar period, broad oceanographic studies of a physical and chemical nature were being conducted off both coasts and in the Gulf of St. Lawrence. By the late 1950s, however, the Board was finding it difficult to fund oceanographic research in addition to the regular fisheries research programs. In 1961, after two years of discussion, the responsibility for the support of all types of shipborne research, including hydrography, was established with the Marine Sciences Branch of the Department of Mines and Technical Surveys. With the exception of the Marine Geological Program which stayed in the Department of Mines and Technical Surveys, the remaining marine research programs and ships were transferred to the new Department of Fisheries and Oceans (DFO) in 1970. In 1973 the Fisheries research establishments and vessels under the Fisheries Research Board became part of DFO's Fisheries and Marine Services which also included oceanographic and hydrographic ships and programs. Fisheries Management in DFO took responsibility for both the Fisheries Conservation and Protection Program (fisheries patrol vessels) and fisheries research vessels. The oceanographic and hydrographic programs and ships formed the Ocean Science and Surveys Program.

In practice, general oceanographic research was originally carried out by the same ships that conducted hydrography. These are listed in Chapter 20. The ships in this chapter were devoted primarily to fisheries research in support of the fishing industry and were assisted by smaller craft that worked in the inshore areas. Commercial trawlers were also chartered from time to time.

A.T. Cameron. DFO

A.T. CAMERON 1958-1982

Builder:	Marine Industries Ltd, Sorel, QC
Date Completed:	1958
Tonnage:	753 (gross)
Dimensions:	177 x 32 x 12.6 (ft) 54 x 9.8 x 3.8 (m)
Machinery:	Single screw controllable pitch diesel, 1000 BHP (746 kW)
Speed:	12 kts

A research vessel of side trawler type built for the Fisheries Research Board, Atlantic Oceanographic Group. Retired 1982, replaced by the *Wilfred Templeman*. Sold (commercial) 1984.

G.B. REED 1962-1990

Builder:	Yarrows Ltd, Victoria, BC
Date Completed:	1962
Tonnage:	768 (gross)
Dimensions:	177.5 x 32 x 12.2 (ft) 54.1 x 9.8 x 3.7 (m)
Machinery:	Single screw controllable pitch diesel, 1000 BHP (746 kW)
Speed:	12 kts

A steel vessel of side trawler type. Named for Dr. Guilford B. Reed, marine biologist and Chairman of the Fisheries Research Board, 1947-1953. The *G.B. Reed* was decommissioned in 1990. Donated to a non-profit organization, repossessed, and finally sold (commercial) in 1997.

E.E. Prince. DFO

E.E. PRINCE 1966-1998

Builder:	Port Weller Drydock Ltd, St.Catharines, ON
Date Completed:	1966
Tonnage:	406 (gross)
Dimensions:	130 x 27 x 12 (ft) 39.7 x 8.3 x 3.65 (m)
Machinery:	Single screw controllable pitch diesel, 600 BHP (440 kW)
Speed:	11 kts

A steel vessel of stern trawler type. Named for Edward E. Prince, Canada's first Commissioner of Fisheries and Chairman of the Fisheries Research Board until 1921. The *E.E. Prince* was based at the Bedford Institute of Oceanography, NS. In reserve 1993. Sold 1998.

Shamook. DFO

MARINUS 1977-1997
SHAMOOK 1975

Builder:	Georgetown Shipyard, PEI
Date Completed:	1975
Tonnage:	117 (gross)
Dimensions:	71 x 22 x 11.5 (ft) 21.6 x 6.7 x 3.5 (m)
Machinery:	Single screw controllable pitch diesel, 480 & 565 BHP (358 & 420 kW)
Speed:	12 kts

Small steel fisheries research vessels. In 1995 *Shamook* was lengthened to 81.7 ft (24.9 m). *Marinus* was taken out of service in 1997 and sold in 1999.

W.E. Ricker. DFO

W.E. RICKER 1986

Builder:	Narasaki Sempakukogyo, Mororan, Japan
Date Completed:	1978
Tonnage:	1105 (gross)
Dimensions:	190 x 31 x 14.8 (ft) 58 x 9.8 x 4.5 (m)
Machinery:	Single screw controllable pitch diesel, 2500 BHP (1863 kW)
Speed:	11.5 kts

A Japanese-built stern trawler, ex *Callistratus*. Purchased 1986 for fisheries research in Pacific waters. Named for W.E. Ricker, Chief Scientist at the Fisheries Research Board, 1966-1973.

Wilfred Templeman. DFO

WILFRED TEMPLEMAN 1981

Builder:	Ferguson Industries Ltd, Pictou, NS
Date Completed:	1981
Tonnage:	925 (gross)
Dimensions:	165 x 36 x 16 (ft) 50.3 x 11 x 4.9 (m)
Machinery:	Single screw controllable pitch diesel 1970 BHP (1470 kW)
Speed:	11 kts

ALFRED NEEDLER 1982

Builder:	Ferguson Industries Ltd, Pictou, NS
Date Completed:	1982
Tonnage:	959 (gross)
Dimensions:	165 x 36 x 16 (ft) 50.3 x 11 x 4.9 (m)
Machinery:	Single screw controllable pitch diesel 3485 BHP (2600 kW)
Speed:	14 kts

Alfred Needler. DFO

Steel stern trawlers of commercial type. Similar ships, except for the difference in machinery, power and speed. The *Wilfred Templeman* is based at St. John's, Nfld and the *Alfred Needler* at the Bedford Institute of Oceanography in Dartmouth, NS. Both are named for distinguished marine biologists.

Calanus II. DFO

CALANUS II 1991

Builder:	Chantier Navale Matane, QC
Date Completed:	1991
Tonnage:	160 (gross)
Dimensions:	65 x 22.6 x 10.5 (ft) 19.9 x 6.9 x 3.2 (m)
Machinery:	Single screw controllable pitch diesel, 675 BHP (503 kW)
Speed:	9.5 kts

A small steel research vessel of stern trawler type.

Teleost. DFO

TELEOST 1993

Builder:	Langsten AS, Tomrefjord, Norway
Date Completed:	1988
Tonnage:	2405 (gross)
Dimensions:	206.5 x 46.6 x 23.6 (ft) 63 x 14.2 x 7.2 (m)
Machinery:	Single screw controllable pitch diesel, 4000 BHP (2985 kW)
Speed:	13.5 kts

A large steel stern trawler, formerly the *Atlantic Champion*, purchased 1993 and converted for fisheries research in 1994. Based in Newfoundland.

CHARTERED VESSELS

The *Lady Hammond* and *Gadus Atlantica* were typical of the commercial trawlers chartered by the department for fisheries research.

Lady Hammond. DFO

Gadus Atlantica. DFO

CHAPTER 20

HYDROGRAPHIC AND OCEANOGRAPHIC SURVEY VESSELS

A t the end of the Second World War, in 1945, there was a great demand for new charts. Little surveying had been done during the war and postwar prosperity and commercial development in new areas on the north shore of the St. Lawrence, in the Great Lakes and in northern Canada, and increased traffic in the "inside passages" in British Columbia, required an expansion of the Canadian Hydrographic Service. The only ships available at the end of hostilities were the *Acadia* on the East Coast and the *Wm. J. Stewart* in British Columbia (Chapter 7). Until a new fleet could be built, former naval vessels were brought into the service. In Pacific waters, the *Marabell,* a yacht that had originally been a USN minesweeper was purchased and a couple of Fishermen's Reserve patrol boats were acquired. On the East Coast, a wooden minesweeper, renamed *Cartier,* was purchased and the *Kapuskasing* and *Fort Frances,* two former RCN fleet minesweepers, were loaned by the Navy. Vessels were also chartered. For northern surveys, it was found that Newfoundland sealing ships were available at the right season and, furthermore, were strengthened for ice and had experienced crews. These included some well known vessels with historic names: *Terra Nova* and *Algerine* among others. One, the *North Star IV,* was lost on an uncharted rock in James Bay in 1960—now called North Star Shoal. These interim vessels sufficed for the first stage of postwar surveying.

In the nineteen fifties and sixties an effective and well balanced hydrographic survey fleet was built up, and all of the new ships were also equipped to carry out oceanographic research. Charting the Arctic regions was a priority and the most capable and impressive of the new vessels were the large ice-strengthened hydrographic and oceanographic ships *Baffin* and *Hudson*, completed in 1956 and 1963, respectively. They were based at the Bedford Institute of Oceanography, near Halifax, which was formally opened in 1962. Two medium-sized near sister ships, the *Parizeau* and *Dawson* (1967/68) were stationed one on each coast and there were two smaller survey vessels, the *Maxwell* (1961) in the east and the *Vector* (1967) in the west. The west coast ships were first based at Victoria and later at the Institute of Ocean Sciences, Sidney, BC. In the Great Lakes the *Limnos* (1968) was built to take over from the Coast Guard crewed *Porte Dauphine* and was assisted by the *Bayfield* (3), a former yacht. These ships operated from the Canada Centre for Inland Waters at Burlington, ON. From time to time, the Coast Guard would also allocate ships for particular surveys, and icebreakers embarked hydrographers for certain Arctic missions.

Much of the actual surveying of harbours and coastal areas was conducted from launches carried by the survey ship. These underwent development during this period and eventually two principal types evolved: seaworthy types with displacement hulls and fast planing craft suited to more sheltered waters. Surveying and navigation systems also became much improved. Accurate, short range electronic systems, erected by the hydrographers for the duration of the survey, and automatic plotting of data as the survey was carried out, speeded up the production of new charts.

The fifties, sixties and seventies were the high period of the hydrographic service. The ships added in the following decade, the *John P. Tully, R.B. Young* and *Matthew*, were modest in size and designed for economical operation, but the additions included very interesting double hulled craft: the *F.C.G. Smith* and *Frederick G. Creed*. The nineties were a time of retrenchment and cutbacks and saw the fleet reduced in numbers. New developments included computerized chart production and the introduction of electronic charts.

Charts must be continuously updated and in spite of all the efforts in the past, many new ones are needed, particularly in the Arctic. This should be the chief challenge for the Canadian Hydrographic Service in the first decades of the present century.

Parry. DFO

PARRY 1947-1969
EKHOLI 1947-1969

Tonnage:	110 (gross)
Dimensions:	84.5 x 20 x 9 (ft)
	25.7 x 6 x 2.7 (m)
Machinery:	Single screw diesel, 360 BHP
Speed:	10 kts

Wooden former coastal patrol vessels of fishing boat design. *Parry* (ex *Talapus*), was used principally for tide and current surveys and *Ekholi* for oceanographic research—both in British Columbia waters.

CARTIER (2) 1947-1968

Builder:	Midland Boat Works, Midland, ON
Date Completed:	1945
Tonnage:	312 (gross)
Dimensions:	140 x 28 x 12.5 (depth) (ft)
	42.7 x 8.5 x 3.8 (m)
Machinery:	Single screw diesel. 550 BHP
Speed:	10 kts

Cartier. DFO

A wooden coastal minesweeper, intended to be named *Ash Lake*. Work on the class ceased at the end of the war, ten completed vessels being transferred to the USSR. *Ash Lake* was purchased in 1947, renamed *Cartier,* and converted for hydrographic service in the Gulf of St Lawrence. In 1962 she transferred to the Great Lakes as a hydrographic training ship, later returning to survey work. Retired 1968.

FORT FRANCES 1948-1958
KAPUSKASING 1949-1972

Built:	Port Arthur, ON
Date Completed:	1944
Tonnage:	1085 (gross)
Dimensions:	225 x 35.5 x 8.6 (ft) 68.6 x 10.8 x 2.6 (m)
Machinery:	Twin screw steam triple expansion, 2700 IHP
Speed:	16 kts

Algerine class fleet minesweepers and escort vessels. Transferred from the RCN in 1948 and 1949 and employed on the East Coast as hydrographic vessels. *Fort Frances* was returned to the Department of National Defence in 1958 and used as a naval auxiliary research vessel. She was scrapped in 1974. *Kapuskasing* was returned in 1972 and, after further service as an auxiliary vessel, was expended as a target in 1978 (see Chapter 21).

Marabell. DFO

MARABELL 1953-1969

Builder:	South Coast Construction, Newport Beach, CA
Date Completed:	1943
Tonnage:	316 (gross)
Dimensions:	136.8 x 24.7 x 10.7 (ft) 41.7 x 7.5 x 3.3 (m)
Machinery:	Twin screw diesel, 1000 BHP (746 kW)
Speed:	11.5 kts

A former USN coastal minesweeper (*YMS-91*), one of a very numerous class. She had been converted to a yacht in 1948. Purchased 1953 for hydrographic service in the Pacific. Sold (commercial) 1969.

Baffin. DFO

BAFFIN 1956-1990

Builder:	Canadian Vickers, Montreal, QC
Date Completed:	1956
Tonnage:	3567 (gross)
Dimensions:	287 x 49.8 x 18.8 (ft) 86.9 x 15.1 x 5.7 (m)
Machinery:	Twin screw diesel, 7060 BHP (5266 kW)
Speed:	15 kts

The first of two large ice-strengthened offshore research and survey ships intended for survey and scientific work in the Arctic, but capable of carrying out a wide range of oceanographic programs. The *Baffin* was fitted with a helicopter deck and hangar and was the first Hydrographic Service ship to carry a helicopter. On her shakedown cruise in 1957 she grounded in the approaches to Shelburne, Nova Scotia, due to an electronic navigation system error, but went on to prove her worth as one of the most comprehensively equipped hydrographic vessels in the world. In the sixties the *Baffin*, along with the *Hudson*, carried out important surveys in the Arctic and transited the Northwest Passage in 1970. She was modernized in 1970, retired in 1990 and sold in 1991.

Baffin. DFO

Hudson. DFO

HUDSON 1963

Builder:	Saint John Shipbuilding and Drydock Ltd, Saint John, NB
Date Completed:	1963
Tonnage:	3740 (gross)
Dimensions:	296.5 x 50.2 x 20.8 (ft) 90.4 x 15.2 x 6.3 (m)
Machinery:	Twin screw diesel-electric, 8670 BHP (6470 kW)
Speed:	17 kts

The second of two large ice-strengthened offshore research and survey ships intended for survey and scientific work in the Arctic, but capable of carrying out a wide range of oceanographic programs. Fitted with a helicopter deck and hangar. From November 1969 to October 1970, the *Hudson* undertook an epic multi-discipline scientific voyage which took her from Nova Scotia to the Antarctic, north through the mid-Pacific and back through the Northwest Passage, the first vessel to circumnavigate both American continents. She was modernized in 1990 and again in 1999.

Hudson. DFO

Maxwell. DFO

MAXWELL 1961-1991

Builder:	Halifax Shipyard Ltd, Halifax, NS
Date Completed:	1961
Tonnage:	244 (gross)
Dimensions:	115 x 25 x 7 (ft) 35 x 7.6 x 2.1 (m)
Machinery:	Twin screw diesel, 700 BHP (522 kW)
Speed:	12 kts

A small steel coastal survey vessel. Named for Staff Commander William Maxwell, a nineteenth century surveyor in the Great Lakes and Newfoundland. Sold (commercial) in 1991.

Vector. DFO

VECTOR 1967

Builder:	Yarrows Ltd, Esquimalt, BC
Date Completed:	1967
Tonnage:	516 (gross)
Dimensions:	130 x 30.7 x 10 (ft) 39.6 x 9.38 x 3.1 (m)
Machinery:	Single screw controllable pitch diesel, 800 BHP (597 kW)
Speed:	12 kts

A steel coastal research and survey vessel. Based at the Institute of Ocean Sciences in Sidney, BC.

Parizeau. DFO

Dawson. DFO

PARIZEAU 1967

Builder:	Burrard Dry Dock Co Ltd, Vancouver, BC
Date Completed:	1967

DAWSON 1968-1992

Builder:	Canadian Vickers Ltd, Montreal, QC
Date Completed:	1968

Specifications for all above:

Tonnage:	1360 (gross)
Dimensions:	212 x 40 x 15 (ft) 64.5 x 12.2 x 4.6 (m)
Machinery:	Twin screw, controllable pitch diesel
Parizeau:	2640 BHP (1967 kW)
Dawson:	3400 BHP (2536 kW)
Speed:	14 kts

Steel offshore research and survey vessels. These ships were named for Henri Delpé Parizeau, Regional Hydrographer, Pacific, 1920-1946, and Dr. W. Bell Dawson, founder, in 1893, of the Canadian Tide and Current Survey. The *Parizeau* was based at the Institute of Ocean Sciences at Sidney, BC until 1991, when she was transferred to the Bedford Institute of Oceanography, Nova Scotia. The *Dawson* was based at the Bedford Institute of Oceanography, Nova Scotia until she was replaced by her sister ship and retired in 1992, only to lie for years gradually deteriorating in Lunenburg harbour. Finally sold as a mother ship for sports fishing boats in 1996.

Limnos. DFO

LIMNOS 1968

Builder:	Port Weller Drydocks Ltd, St. Catharines, ON
Date Completed:	1968
Tonnage:	460 (gross)
Dimensions:	147 x 32 x 8.5 (ft) 44.8 x 9.75 x 2.6 (m)
Machinery:	Twin screw (directional drive) diesel. 1000 BHP (750 kW)
Speed:	10 kts

A steel coastal research and survey vessel based at the Canada Centre for Inland Waters in Burlington, ON. Originally intended to support hydrographic surveys and limnological research (the study of freshwater lakes), she has been employed almost entirely in the latter discipline.

Bayfield. DFO

BAYFIELD (3) 1974-1991

Builder:	Kristiansands Mek. Werks A.S., Kristiansand, Norway
Date Completed:	1960
Tonnage:	178 (gross)
Dimensions:	105.6 x 21 x 8.8 (ft) 32.2 x 6.4 x 2.7 (m)
Machinery:	Twin screw diesel, 580 BHP (433 kW)
Speed:	10 kts

The *Bayfield* was built as a marine biological research vessel. Her original name was *Vicca*. She was converted to a private yacht by the Eaton family and renamed *Hildur* in 1972. Purchased by the Department of the Environment in 1974 and became the third hydrographic ship named for Admiral Henry Wolsey Bayfield. Employed on hydrographic programs and scientific research in the Great Lakes. Sold (commercial) 1991.

Louis M. Lauzier. DFO

LOUIS M. LAUZIER (ex CAPE HARRISON)

1983

Builder:	Breton Industries Ltd, Port Hawkesbury, NS
Date Completed:	1976
Tonnage:	322 (gross)
Dimensions:	124 x 27 x 6.9 (ft) 37.1 x 8.2 x 2.13 (m)
Machinery:	Twin screw diesel 1600 BHP (1200 kW)
Speed:	12.5 kts

An aluminium coastal research and survey vessel originally the fisheries patrol vessel *Cape Harrison* (see Chapter 18). Converted to a survey and research vessel in 1983 and renamed in honour of Dr. Louis Lauzier, a distinguished oceanographer. Her main engines were replaced by more economical units. Employed in the Gulf of St. Lawrence until 1991, she was then transferred to the Canada Centre for Inland Waters at Burlington. She was taken out of service in 1995 and has been on charter to the Memorial University of Newfoundland since 1998.

John P. Tully. DFO

JOHN P. TULLY 1985

Builder:	Bel-Air Shipyard Ltd, Vancouver, BC
Date Completed:	1985
Tonnage:	2021 (gross)
Dimensions:	226 x 46 x 14.8 (ft) 68.9 x 14.5 x 4.5 (m)
Machinery:	Single screw controllable pitch diesel, 3700 BHP (2757 kW)
Speed:	13.5 kts

An offshore research and survey vessel, very similar to the fisheries patrol vessel *Leonard J. Cowley*. Named for distinguished hydrographer, John P. Tully. She is based at the Institute of Ocean Sciences at Sidney, BC.

F.C.G. Smith. DFO

F.C.G. SMITH 1985

Builder:	Georgetown Shipyard, PEI
Date Completed:	1985
Tonnage:	438.(gross)
Dimensions:	114 x 46 x 6.9 (ft) 34.8 x 14 x 2.1 (m)
Machinery:	Twin screw controllable pitch diesel 800 BHP (596 kW)
Speed:	10 kts

A steel, double hulled, survey and sounding vessel, named for F.C. Goulding Smith, Dominion Hydrographer 1952-57. The width of the sweep is increased by booms equipped with multi-channel transducers, interfaced with a precision electronic navigation system. Employed on surveys in the Maritimes until 1995 when she was transferred to the Laurentian Region where she is deployed on surveys of the St. Lawrence Seaway.

F.C.G. Smith. DFO

R.B. Young. DFO

R.B. YOUNG 1990

Builder:	Allied Shipbuilders, North Vancouver, BC
Date Completed:	1990
Tonnage:	300 (gross)
Dimensions:	105 x 26 x 7.5 (ft) 32.3 x 8 x 2.3 (m)
Machinery:	Twin screw controllable pitch diesel 1300 BHP (960 kW)
Speed:	11.5 kts

A steel coastal research and survey vessel, named for Robert B. Young, Regional Hydrographer, Pacific, 1953-1968. The ship is based at the Institute of Ocean Sciences at Sidney, BC.

MATTHEW 1990

Builder:	Versatile Pacific Shipyards, Inc., North Vancouver, BC
Date Completed:	1990
Tonnage:	857 (gross)
Dimensions:	165 x 34.4 x 14 (ft) 50.3 x 10.5 x 4.3 (m)
Machinery:	Twin screw controllable pitch diesel. 1810 BHP (1350 kW)
Speed:	12 kts

A steel coastal research and survey vessel. Named for John Cabot's ship of 1497. Based at the Bedford Institute of Oceanography, NS.

Matthew. C.D. Maginley (Private Collection)

Frederick G. Creed. Charles Maginley (Private collection)

FREDERICK G. CREED 1994

Builder:	Swath Ocean Systems Inc., San Diego, CA
Date Completed:	1988
Tonnage:	152 (gross)
Dimensions:	67 x 32 x 8.5 (ft) 20.4 x 9.75 x 2.6 (m)
Machinery:	Twin screw diesel, 2150 BHP (1610 kW)
Speed:	21 kts

An aluminium, double hulled, survey and sounding vessel, built on the SWATH (small waterplane area, twin hull) concept. Purchased 1994. Named for the originator of the SWATH design, a native of Nova Scotia. Fitted with exceptionally accurate positioning systems and employed on precision surveys in the Laurentian and Maritime Regions. She has carried out wave dynamics studies off Cape Hatteras and North Carolina which were designed around the vessel's unique capabilities.

CHAPTER 21
NAVAL AUXILIARY VESSELS

T he Canadian Naval Auxiliary Service came into being at the end of the Second World War. During the war, auxiliary vessels, including tugs and harbour craft, had naval crews but in peacetime a reduced Navy could not spare personnel for these tasks. In the closing days of the war, the Queen's Harbour Master, Captain O.C.S. Robertson (who later was the first commanding officer of the navy's icebreaker HMCS *Labrador*) proposed the creation of a civilian auxiliary fleet. Naval Headquarters agreed, and the Canadian Naval Auxiliary Service was organised in late 1945, becoming fully effective in May 1946. In many cases, there was no change to the crews of existing vessels—the naval crews of the yard craft were demobilised and came back to do the same job as civilians.

At first the auxiliary fleet was comprised mainly of tugs, lighters and similar harbour craft, but there were also two coastal supply vessels and two tankers that had accommodation for their crew, together with the *Whitethroat*, which was used to maintain submarine detection loops and cables. From 1953, the service operated research vessels. At first these were former naval craft like the corvette *Sackville* and four converted minesweepers, but in the 1960s purpose-built research ships, the *Endeavour* and *Quest,* were added to the fleet.

The tasks assigned to these ships could be divided into two main areas: purely scientific oceanographic research and research specifically directed towards the detection of submarines. In some cases, the two overlapped—the physical oceanography and geology of the Gulf of St. Lawrence and the continental shelf had application not only to submarine detection but to resource development. Studies of the propagation of sound under water were related to the installation of long range passive submarine detection systems on the seabed. At Shelburne, NS and later at Argentia, Newfoundland, the RCN operated stations in the chain of underwater surveillance installations known as SOSUS. Another area of investigation was the active sonar detection of submarines by variable depth sonar. This resulted in towed sonar transmitters being fitted to modified St. Laurent class destroyers.

The scientific establishments which directed these researches were: the Atlantic Oceanographic Group (AOG), at St. Andrews, NB, and the Naval Research Establishment (NRE), Dartmouth, which became the Defence Research Establishment Atlantic (DREA) and its West Coast equivalent. Naval Auxiliary research ships were often lent to or employed by other government departments, especially Mines and Technical Surveys (later Fisheries and Oceans). Along with the hydrographic and oceanographic ships shown in the previous chapter, they conducted various programs for the Bedford Institute of Oceanography (BIO) and the research group on the west coast which eventually became the Institute for Ocean Sciences (IOS). Non-government civilian agencies that used these ships included the Institute of Oceanography of Dalhousie University and the University of British Columbia.

These civilian-crewed Department of Defence ships and craft are known as Canadian Naval Auxiliary Vessels (CNAVs). The letter and number designations after the ships' names were assigned in accordance with a system agreed to by NATO. Examples: Tug—ATA; Cargo ship, small—AKS; Oiler, Coastal—AOC; Oceanographic Research vessel—AGOR.

Cedarwood. MCM

Research Vessels

CEDARWOOD (AKS 530 then AGH 530)

1946-1948 and 1956-1959

Builder:	Smith and Rhuland, Lunenburg, NS
Date Completed:	1941
Tonnage:	566 tons displacement.
Dimensions:	166 x 30.5 x 10 (ft) 50.6 x 9.3 x 3 (m)
Machinery:	Single screw diesel, 600 BHP
Speed:	11 kts

A wooden vessel built as the coastal freighter *J.E. Kinney*, but taken over by the Army Service Corps for supplying army bases in Newfoundland and renamed *General Schmidlin*. In 1946 she became a Naval Auxiliary Vessel and was transferred to the West Coast. From September 1948 to October 1956 she was in commission in the Navy and used for oceanographic surveys on the West Coast (the photo shows her in naval service). She again became a CNAV until May 1958, when she was converted into a replica of the pioneer paddle steamer *Beaver*. She also impersonated the *Commodore*, the first ship to bring miners to BC from San Francisco. Sold (commercial) in 1959.

WHITETHROAT (NPC 113, then AGH 113)
1946-1951 and 1954-1967

Builder:	Cook, Welton and Gemmell, Beverly, England
Date Completed:	1944
Tonnage:	580 tons displacement
Dimensions:	164 x 27.5 x 12.5 (ft) 50 x 8.4 x 3.8 (m)
Machinery:	Single screw steam triple expansion, 850 IHP
Speed:	12.5 kts

An Isles class trawler converted to a controlled mine layer. In 1946 she became a Canadian Naval Auxiliary Vessel with a civilian crew and in 1947 was employed making repairs to submarine cables. *Whitethroat* was used for oceanographic research in 1950-51 but was then re-commissioned in the Navy as a mine layer until 1954, when she again reverted to the auxiliary service. In 1955 her duties were taken over by the new *Bluethroat* and she was transferred to the Pacific Command where she continued to work as a CNAV, performing various research and scientific tasks and planting practice mines for RCN minesweepers to clear during minesweeping exercises. *Whitethroat* was sold in 1967.

Sackville. Marc Milner (Private Collection)

SACKVILLE (ALC 113, then AGOR 113)
1953-1982

Sackville. MCM

Builder:	Saint John Dry Dock, Saint John, NB
Date Completed:	1941
Tonnage:	1085 tons displacement.
Dimensions:	205 x 33 x 14.5 (ft) 62.5 x 10.1 x 4.4 (m)
Machinery:	Single screw steam triple expansion, c.1400 IHP (One boiler removed during conversion)
Speed:	14 kts

One of the numerous Canadian corvettes, the mainstay of the anti-submarine forces during the first part of the anti-submarine war. After very active service in the North Atlantic, she was selected for conversion to a loop layer. Work started in November 1944 and completed in May 1945, when the ship was put to work removing submarine detection loops from the approaches to East Coast ports. On completion of this task she was placed in reserve. In 1953 she was reactivated and became a Naval Auxiliary Vessel. Her first assignment was oceanographic research in the Gulf of St. Lawrence under the direction of the Atlantic Oceanographic Group (AOG) based at St. Andrews, NB. Over the next twenty-nine years she worked on a variety of scientific projects, some civilian, some military. During this long period she was progressively modified and at the end of her career, with a new bridge structure and a prominent laboratory aft, she was scarcely recognisable as a corvette.

As her career drew to an end, various groups and museums became interested in preserving *Sackville*, the last surviving example of the many corvettes built in Canada during the Second World War. In the end, an organisation known as the Canadian Naval Corvette Trust assumed ownership, the Maritime Museum of the Atlantic in Halifax provided the venue for displaying the ship and the Navy provided support for restoration, docking and winter maintenance. By 1984 she had been converted to her wartime configuration, at least externally and was opened to the public in the summer of 1985. In subsequent years, original equipment and weapons were found and put in place. She is now berthed at Sackville Landing, Halifax, and is open to visitors during the summer months.

BLUETHROAT (NPC 114, then AGOR 114)

1955-1990

Builder:	Geo. W. Davie and Sons Ltd, Lauzon, QC
Date Completed:	1955
Tonnage:	785 tons displacement
Dimensions:	157 x 33 x 10 (ft) 47.9 x 10.1 x 3 (m)
Machinery:	Twin screw diesel 1200 BHP
Speed:	13 kts

Built as a mine layer and loop layer but converted to a research vessel in 1964. Employed on oceanographic research for the usual military and civilian research agencies and laboratories (AOG, BIO, NRE and DREA). She also deployed with the active fleet to the Caribbean and was used as a stores ship during spring training cruises. Replaced by *Riverton* (2).

New Liskeard. MCM

OSHAWA (AGOR 174) 1958-1966
NEW LISKEARD (AGOR 168) 1958-1969
FORT FRANCES (AGOR 170) 1958-1974
KAPUSKASING (AGOR 173) 1972-1975

Builder:	Port Arthur Shipbuilding Co, Port Arthur, ON
Date Completed:	1943
Tonnage:	1040 tons displacement
Dimensions:	235.5 x 35.5 x 11 (ft) 71.8 x 10.8 x 3.4 (m)
Machinery:	Twin screw steam triple expansion, 2000 IHP
Speed:	16.5 kts

Fort Frances. MCM

Algerine class minesweepers and escort vessels that proved useful as research and hydrographic vessels. *Oshawa* was placed in reserve postwar but in 1957-58 was converted for oceanographic research on the West Coast and reactivated as a CNAV. She was replaced by *Endeavour* in 1965 and broken up in 1966. *New Liskeard* was employed postwar as a training ship and subsequently for research, but still under the white ensign. In 1958, after further conversion, she became a CNAV and so served until 1969, when she was replaced by *Quest* and sold for breaking up. *Fort Frances* and a sister ship, *Kapuskasing*, were loaned to the Department of Mines and Natural Resources in 1948 and were used as hydrographic survey vessels. In 1958 *Fort Frances* was returned to the Department of National Defence and refitted with modern laboratories and extra accommodation. From 1959 she was employed on defence related research work. She was sold for breaking up in 1974. *Kapuskasing* remained with the Canadian Hydrographic Service until 1972 and then served a further three years in Pacific waters as a CNAV. She was sunk as a target in 1978.

Endeavour. MCM

ENDEAVOUR (AGOR 171) 1965-2000

Builder:	Yarrows Ltd, Esquimalt, BC
Date Completed:	1965
Tonnage:	1560 tons displacement
Dimensions:	236 x 38.5 x 13 (ft) 71.9 x 11.7 x 4 (m)
Machinery:	Twin screw diesel-electric, 5600 SHP (4175 kW)
Speed:	16 kts

A purpose-built naval research vessel designed for anti-submarine research. Fitted with a helicopter deck. *Endeavour* replaced *Oshawa* and was stationed on the West Coast until 1999 when she temporarily relieved *Quest* on the East Coast during that ship's modernisation. In 2000 she was placed on the disposal list.

Quest. MCM

QUEST (AGOR 172) 1969

Builder:	Burrard Dry Dock Co, Vancouver, BC
Date Completed:	1969
Tonnage:	2130 tons displacement
Dimensions:	235 x 42 x 15.5 (ft) 71.6 x 12.8 x 4.6 (m)
Machinery:	Twin screw diesel electric, 5600 SHP (4175 kW)
Speed:	16 kts

A development of the *Endeavour* design, *Quest* is an ice-strengthened naval research vessel. She is fitted with a helicopter deck. *Quest* replaced *New Liskeard* and is used for defence related oceanographic research. She is based at Halifax.

Riverton. MCM

RIVERTON (2) (AG 121) 1989-1997

Builder:	De Waal, Netherlands
Date Completed:	1975
Tonnage:	2563 tons displacement
Dimensions:	209 x 43.5 x 16.5 (ft) 63.9 x 13.3 x 5.1 (m)
Machinery:	Twin screw diesel, 10100 BHP (1742 kW)
Speed:	15.5 kts

An offshore supply and support vessel, formerly *Smit-Lloyd 112*, acquired in 1989 and, in theory, replaced *Bluethroat*, although she is nothing like that vessel. She was used principally during the trials of the Halifax class frigates that were completed between 1992 and 1997 and probably towed large acoustic arrays. On completion of the frigate program she was bareboat chartered to Secunda Marine, but is still owned by the Department of National Defence.

Coastal Cargo Vessels

EASTORE (AKS 515) 1946-1964
LAYMORE (AKS 516, then AGOR 516)
1946-1977

Built :	Brunswick, GA
Date Completed:	1944
Tonnage:	560 (gross)
Dimensions:	176.5 x 32 x 8 9 (ft) 53.8 x 9.8 x 2.7 (m)
Machinery:	Single screw diesel, 1000 BHP
Speed:	10.8 kts

Small coastal cargo vessels of US Army design. Originally they were commissioned vessels, both serving on the East Coast but in 1946 they hoisted the blue ensign as CNAVs and *Laymore* was then transferred to the Pacific. They were used to supply outlying bases such as Shelburne, Nova Scotia and Nanoose, British Columbia. *Eastore* was sold in 1964. *Laymore* became a research vessel in 1966 and was sold in 1977.

Dundalk. MCM

Coastal Tankers

DUNDALK (AOC 501) 1946-1983
DUNDURN (AOC 502) 1948-1985

Builder:	Canadian Bridge Co, Walkerville, ON
Date Completed:	1943
Tonnage:	950 tons displacement
Dimensions:	178.8 x 32.2 x 13 (ft)
Machinery:	Single screw diesel, 700 BHP
Speed:	10 kts

Small coastal tankers, used to refuel warships in harbour and to deliver fuel to outlying bases. Originally commissioned vessels based at Halifax, they became CNAVs in 1946. In 1947 *Dundurn* was transferred to the Pacific and was based at Esquimalt. *Dundalk* was sold (commercial) in 1983 and was wrecked in the West Indies in 1985. *Dundurn* was sold in 1985.

Tugs

HEATHERTON
(ATA 527) 1946-1975

Builder:	Montreal Dry Dock, QC

RIVERTON (1)
(ATA 528) 1946-1978

Builder:	Chantier Maritime, St. Laurent, QC

CLIFTON (ATA 529) 1946-1977

Builder:	Canadian Bridge Co Walkerville, ON

Specifications for all:

Tonnage:	462 tons displacement
Dimensions:	112 x 28 x 11 (ft)
Machinery:	Single screw diesel, 1000 BHP
Speed:	11 kts

These large harbour tugs had naval crews in wartime and became auxiliary vessels in 1946. Another, *Beaverton*, was lost by collision, in the St. Lawrence River in 1946 during delivery from Montreal Dry Dock. There was loss of life, including Lt.Cdr Richards, the senior CNAV pilot. *Heatherton* was transferred to the Department of Public Works in 1975. *Riverton* and *Clifton* were sold (commercial) in 1978 and 1977 respectively.

SAINT ANTHONY
(ATA 531) 1957-1994
SAINT CHARLES
(ATA 533) 1957-1994
SAINT JOHN
(ATA 535) 1957-1971

Builder:	Saint John Dry Dock Company, Saint John, NB
Date Completed:	1957
Tonnage:	840 tons displacement
Dimensions:	151.5 x 33 x 17 (ft)
Machinery:	Single screw diesel, 1920 BHP
Speed:	14 kts

Saint Charles. MCM

Supposedly ocean going tugs, but a very low freeboard made work on the after deck difficult. Duties included target towing and they were sometimes deployed with the fleet on exercises. *Saint John* was the first to be sold, in 1971. She sank off Labrador in 1980 while in commercial service as *Dolphin X*. The other two were sold in 1994.

Glenevis. MCM

Smaller Harbour Tugs

Smaller tugs for harbour use had names beginning with "Glen". The older type, of conventional tug design, was replaced in 1975-77 by new tugs with Voith-Schneider propulsion. Fire-fighting tugs were also in the inventory.

Glendyne. DND IXC84-578

CHAPTER 22

MISCELLANEOUS VESSELS

T his chapter includes research and survey vessels, sounding vessels needed for verifying the depths in the St. Lawrence ship channel, a bait ship, the Coast Guard College training ship, (a former light vessel), a chartered icebreaking tug and representative lightships.

Glenada. DFO

Survey and Sounding Vessels

GLENADA 1946-1973

Builder:	Russel Bros, Owen Sound, ON
Date Completed:	1943
Tonnage:	101 (gross)
Dimensions:	73 x 20 x 7.5 (ft) 22.2 x 6.1 x 2.3 (m)
Machinery:	Single screw diesel, 320 BHP (238 kW)
Speed:	10 kts

One of the steel naval harbour tugs of the Glen class. Used as a survey vessel and for general duties in the canal and seaway system. Sold 1973.

Porte Dauphine. DFO

PORTE DAUPHINE

1960-1974

Builder:	Pictou Foundry, Pictou, NS
Date Completed:	1952
Tonnge:	347 (gross)
Dimensions:	119.5 x 26 x 11 (ft) 36.4 x 7.9 x 3.35 (m)
Machinery:	Single screw diesel, 600 IHP (448 kW)
Speed:	10 kts

A steel naval "gate vessel" of side trawler type, on loan from the RCN as an environmental research vessel in the Great Lakes. Returned to the Navy in 1974.

Ville Marie. DFO

VILLE MARIE 1960-1986

Builder:	Russel-Hipwell, Owen Sound, ON
Date Completed:	1960
Tonnage:	390 (gross)
Dimensions:	134 x 18 x 10 (ft) 40.9 x 8.5 x 2.9 (m)
Machinery:	Twin screw diesel-electric, 1000 SHP (746 kW)
Speed:	13 kts

A steel survey vessel for the St. Lawrence ship channel. The smallest diesel-electric vessel in the fleet. In 1980 she was converted to a search and rescue cutter and stationed in the Laurentian Region. Sold 1986 and became a youth training vessel.

Beauport. DFO

BEAUPORT 1960-1988

Builder:	Davie Shipbuilding Ltd, Lauzon, QC
Date Completed:	1960
Tonnage:	813 (gross)
Dimensions:	167 x 34 x 9 (ft) 51.1 x 7.3 x 2.7 (m)
Machinery:	Twin screw diesel, 1280 SHP (955 kW)
Speed:	13 kts

A steel sounding vessel for the St. Lawrence ship channel, a modern version of the old *Detector* of 1915. (See Chapter 8) Decommissioned 1988. Sold 1989.

NICOLET 1966-1995

Builder:	Collingwood Shipbuilding, Collingwood, ON
Date Completed:	1966
Tonnage:	887 (gross)
Dimensions:	166.5 x 35 x 9.6 (ft) 50.8 x 10.7 x 2.9 (m)
Machinery:	Twin screw diesel, 1660 SHP (1240 kW)
Speed:	13 kts

A steel sounding vessel for the St. Lawrence ship channel, very similar to the *Beauport*. Sold 1995.

Arctica. DFO

Bait ship

ARCTICA 1964-1981

Builder:	Davie Shipbuilding Ltd, Lauzon, QC
Date Completed:	1964
Tonnage:	702 (gross)
Dimensions:	166 x 32.5 x 11.7 (ft) 50.6 x 9.9 x 3.6 (m)
Machinery:	Single screw diesel, 1280 BHP (955 kW)
Speed:	10 kts

A small freighter used to deliver fresh and frozen bait to outports in Newfoundland, operated by the Fisheries Management branch.

Training Ship

MIKULA (2) 1972-1994

Builder:	Kingston Shipyard, Kingston, ON
Date Completed:	1959
Tonnage:	526 (gross)
Dimensions:	128 x 30.5 x 11 (ft) 39 x 9.3 x 3.4 (m)
Machinery:	Single screw diesel, 372 BHP (277 kW)
Speed:	9.5 kts

Originally Lightship No.4. Used chiefly on the Lurcher shoal on the southwest coast of Nova Scotia. When crewed lightships were replaced by large offshore light buoys, No. 4 was converted (1972) for service as a training ship for the Coast Guard College in Sydney, and was given the name of the pre-war icebreaker *Mikula* (see Chapter 3). Sold (commercial) 1994.

NOTE: The small buoy tenders *Skidegate* and *Robert Foulis* were also used as College training ships for briefer periods.

Arctik Ivik. J.P.G. St-Pierre (Private Collection)

Icebreaking tug (chartered)

ARCTIC IVIK 1993-1996

Builder:	Allied Shipbuilders, North Vancouver, BC
Date Completed:	1985
Tonnage:	1564 (gross)
Dimensions:	224.3 x 47.5 x 16 (ft) 68.4 x 14.5 x 4.9 (m)
Machinery:	Twin screw diesel, 10800 BHP (8056 kW)
Speed:	15 kts

A powerful icebreaking tug chartered by the Coast Guard from August 1993 to May 1996 for operations in the Western Arctic and also used for search and rescue on the West Coast.

Lightships

Lightship No.1 Sambro. DFO

LIGHTSHIP No. 1 (SAMBRO)

An example of postwar lightships with large tripod masts to support the light. The Sambro station marks the entrance to Halifax harbour. In the 1970s, lightships were replaced by large light buoys with continuous audio signals activated by the buoys' motion in the waves.

LIGHTSHIP No. 2 (LURCHER)

A postwar lightship, completed in 1957. The name on the side is the name of the station, not the ship. The Lurcher shoal is off the southwest coast of Nova Scotia and the lightship was an important navigation aid for vessels entering the Bay of Fundy. No. 2 was eventually used as an alongside engineering training facility at the Coast Guard College in Sydney, NS, while Lightship No. 4, which replaced her on the Lurcher shoal, became the seagoing training ship *Mikula*. (See above.)

Lightship No.2 Lurcher. DFO

CHAPTER 23
HOVERCRAFT

Air cushion vehicles (ACVs) or hovercraft were initially put into service in the late 1960s as search and rescue units based at the Vancouver airport. They could operate with equal facility over water and over the extensive mudflats at the mouth of the Fraser River and soon proved their worth. In 1972, a larger and heavier type of hovercraft, the *Voyageur*, was tried on the Mackenzie River and the Arctic and Great Lakes. Eventually this craft went into service on the St. Lawrence River and was used for servicing navigation aids, many of which were placed on sandbars or in shallow water areas where the hovercraft's amphibious capability made it an ideal vehicle for the purpose. It was also found that sheets of ice, typical of those that formed in the wider portions of the river, could be broken by an ACV. From 1987, new designs of hovercraft, economically powered by diesel engines, came into service and were deployed on both coasts, replacing the older units.

CG-021. DFO

CG 021 1968-1984
CG 039 1977-1998
CG 045 1982
CG 086 1986-1993

Builder:	British Hovercraft, Cowes, IOW, England
Tonnage:	8 tons
Machinery:	One gas-turbine (1100 kW)
Speed:	55 kts

CG 021 was a Type SRN 5. The others were the somewhat longer Type SRN 6.

CG 021 and *039* were acquired in 1968 and 1977 respectively. *CG 045* and *CG 086* were purchased in 1981 as spares, but were re-built and entered service some years later. Used for search and rescue, based at Vancouver and Parksville, BC. Retired on the dates shown.

CG-045. DFO

Voyageur. DFO

VOYAGEUR 1972-1987

Builder:	Bell Aerospace Canada Ltd, Grand Bend, ON
Date Completed:	1972
Tonnage:	48 tons
Machinery:	Two gas-turbines (1940 kW)
Speed:	50 kts

After trials in the Great Lakes and the Arctic, the *Voyageur* was used principally for servicing navigation aids in the Laurentian Region. Retired 1987.

Waban Aki. DFO

WABAN-AKI 1987

Builder:	British Hovercraft, Cowes. IOW, England
Date Completed:	1987
Tonnage:	28 tons
Machinery:	Four diesels, (1760 kW)
Speed :	50 kts

Replaced the *Voyageur* in the Laurentian Region. Used for icebreaking and servicing navigation aids.

SIPU-MUIN, SIYÄY 1998

Builder:	Hike Metal Products, Wheatley, ON
Date Completed:	1998
Tonnage:	35 tons
Machinery:	Four diesels, (2818 kW)
Speed:	50 kts

Sipu-muin is based in the Laurentian Region as a navigation aids craft and icebreaker. *Siyäy* is based in British Columbia for servicing navigation aids and for search and rescue duties. These two ACVs are the largest diesel-powered hovercraft in the world.

INDEX OF SHIPS

(Note: Names of ships that are described in the book are shown in **bold** type)

A.T. Cameron — Fisheries research vessel, 231

Aberdeen — Lighthouse supply vessel and buoy tender, 49

Acadia (1) — Fisheries patrol vessel, 84

Acadia (2) — Hydrographic survey vessel, 102, 141

Admiral — Pre-confederation steamer, 20

Advance — Pre-confederation steamer, 20

Adversus — Customs and RCMP patrol vessel, 77

Aigle d'Ocean — Freighter, formerly tug *Ocean Eagle*, 112

Aklavik — Hudson Bay Company Schooner, 115

Alachasse — Customs and RCMP patrol vessel, 77

Alberni — Lighthouse supply vessel and buoy tender, 60

Alert (1) — Northern exploration vessel, 28

Alert (2) — Search and Rescue cutter, 206

Alexander Henry — Light icebreaker and navigation aids tender, 172

Alexander Mackenzie — Navigation aids tender, 184

Alfred Needler — Fisheries research vessel, 235

Algerine — Chartered survey vessel, 239

Ann Harvey — Light icebreaker and navigation aids tender, 125, 176

Aranmore — Lighthouse supply vessel and buoy tender, 56

Arctic — Northern patrol vessel, 30

Arctic Ivik — Icebreaking tug, 275

Arctic Prowler — Seismic vessel, formerly *Cygnus (2)*, 222

Arctica — Bait vessel, 273

Argenteuil — Ottawa River buoy tender, 66

Arleux — Fisheries patrol vessel, 91, 113

Arras — Fisheries patrol vessel, 91, 113

Arrow Post — Fisheries patrol vessel, 229

Arun — British lifeboat type, 212

Ash Lake — Minesweeper—became *Cartier (2)*, 241

Auk — Northern supply vessel, 201

Baffin — Hydrographic & oceanographic vessel, 244

Baffin Service — Offshore supply vessel, 208

Bar Off — Customs patrol vessel, former rum runner, 73

Bartlett — Ice-strengthened navigation aids vessel, 182

Bayfield (1) — Hydrographic survey vessel, 97

Bayfield (2) — Hydrographic survey vessel, 78, 98

Bayfield (3) — Great Lakes research vessel, 249

Bayhound — Customs patrol vessel, former yacht, 75

Bear — US Coast Guard cutter, 31

Beauharnois — Formerly *Richelieu*, 19

Beauport — Sounding vessel, 271, 272

Beaver — Hudson Bay Company steamer, 64, 257

Beaverton — Naval auxiliary tug, 267

Bellechasse — Survey and inspection vessel, 107

Beothic — Chartered northern patrol vessel, 30, 114

Bernier — Lighthouse supply vessel and buoy tender, 68

Berthier — Survey and inspection vessel, 108

Bickerton — Self righting lifeboat, 135, 212

Blue Heron — RCMP patrol vessel, 216

Bluethroat — Naval Auxiliary vessel, 260

Bo Peep — Rum runner—became *Bar Off*, 73

Brant (1) — Small buoy tender, 62

Brant (2) — Lighthouse supply vessel and buoy tender, 68

C. D. Howe — Eastern Arctic patrol ship, 146

C. P. Edwards — Navigation aids tender, 183

Calanus II — Fisheries research vessel, 236

Callistratus — Trawler—became *W.E. Ricker*, 234

Camsell — Light icebreaker and navigation aids vessel, 170

Canada — Fisheries patrol vessel, 89

Canso — DPW tug used for Customs patrol, 78

Cape Breton — Dominion Coal Company steamer, 85

Cape Calvert — Self righting lifeboat, 212

Cape Freels — Fisheries patrol vessel, 223

Cape Harrison	Fisheries patrol vessel—became *Louis M. Lauzier*, 226, 250
Cape Hurd	Small search and rescue cutter, 211
Cape Roger	Fisheries patrol vessel, 225
Cape St. James	Self righting lifeboat, 212
Cape Sutil	Self righting lifeboat, 212
Caribou Isle	Small buoy tender, 191
Cartier (1)	Hydrographic survey vessel, 78, 100
Cartier (2)	Hydrographic survey vessel, 241
Cathy B	Offshore supply vessel—became *George E. Darby*, 207
Cedarwood	Naval Auxiliary survey vessel, 257
CG021, 039, 045, 086	Hovercraft, 278
Champlain	Icebreaker, 38
Charmer	C.P.R. vessel, 48
Charny	Formerly *Cartier (1)*, 100
Chebucto	Fisheries patrol vessel, 223
Chesterfield	Lighthouse supply vessel and buoy tender, 61
Chrissie C. Thomey	Hydrographic survey schooner, 96
Christine	Customs patrol vessel, 71
Citadelle	Fire fighting tug, later pilot vessel, 112
Cleveland Amory	Protest ship, formerly *Thomas Carleton*, 180
Clifton	Naval Auxiliary tug, 267
Coal Barge No. 7	Became *Alberni*, 60
Columbia	Yacht, became *Stadacona*, 103
Concretia	Ferro-cement buoy tender, 66
Conestoga	Customs patrol vessel, former yacht, 74
Constance	Customs and fisheries patrol vessel, 71, 86
Contralmirante Oscar Viel Toro	Formerly *Norman Mcleod Rogers*, 153
Cove Isle	Small buoy tender, 190
Curlew	Fisheries patrol vessel, 86
CURV II	USN recovery vehicle, 160
Cygnus (1)	Fisheries patrol vessel, 220
Cygnus (2)	Fisheries patrol vessel, 222
Cygnus (3)	Fisheries patrol vessel, 225
D'Iberville	Icebreaker, 123, 133, 149
Daring (2)	Search and rescue cutter, 207
Dawson	Hydrographic & oceanographic vessel, 247
Des Groseilliers	Icebreaker, 154
Detector	Sounding vessel, 108, 272
Diana	Chartered survey vessel, 29
Dollard	Lighthouse supply vessel and buoy tender, 56, 78
Dolphin X	Formerly *Saint John*, 267
Doris	Pre-confederation steamer, 20
Druid (1)	Pre-confederation steamer, 22
Druid (2)	Lighthouse supply vessel and buoy tender, 50
Dumit (1)	Special river navigation aids tender, 193
Dumit (2)	Special river navigation aids tender, 197
Dundalk	Naval Auxiliary tanker, 266
Dundurn	Naval Auxiliary tanker, 266
E.E. Prince	Fisheries research vessel, 233
Earl Grey (1)	Icebreaker, 40
Earl Grey (2)	Light icebreaker and navigation aids tender, 175
Eastore	Naval Auxiliary cargo vessel, 265
Eckaloo (1)	Special river navigation aids tender, 129, 194
Eckaloo (2)	Special river navigation aids tender, 198
Edsall	Tug, became *Gen. U.S. Grant*, then *Bayfield (1)*, 97
Edward	Formerly *Edward Cornwallis (1)*, 166
Edward Cornwallis (1)	Ice-strengthened navigation aids vessel, 166
Edward Cornwallis (2)	Light icebreaker and navigation aids tender, 177
Eider	Northern supply vessel, 201
Ekholi	Small hydrographic survey vessel, 241
Endeavour	Naval Auxiliary research vessel, 262
Ernest Lapointe	Icebreaker, 44, 132
Estevan	Lighthouse supply vessel and buoy tender, 55
F.C.G. Smith	Hydrographic survey and sounding vessel, 252
Fedor Litke	Soviet icebreaker, formerly *Earl Grey (1)*, 40
Firebird	Naval auxiliary tug, 143
Fleur de lis	Customs and RCMP patrol vessel, 76
Fort Frances	Hydrographic and Naval Auxiliary research vessel, 242, 261
Fort Pitt	RCMP patrol vessel, 215
Fort Selkirk	RCMP patrol vessel (not commissioned), 215
Fort Steel	RCMP patrol vessel (not commissioned), 215

Fort Steele	RCMP patrol vessel, 215	
Fort Walsh	RCMP patrol vessel, 215	
Foxhound	Became *La Canadienne (2)*, 84, 101	
Fram	Nansen's arctic exploration vessel, 30	
Franklin (1)	Lighthouse supply vessel and buoy tender, 60	
Franklin (2)	Icebreaker—became *Sir John Franklin*, 154	
Frederick G. Creed	Hydrographic survey vessel, 254	
French (1)	RCMP patrol vessel, 80	
French (2)	RCMP patrol vessel, 210	
Frontenac	Survey and inspection vessel, 109	
Fylgia	Wrecked steamer, 21	
G.B. Reed	Fisheries research vessel, 232	
Gadus Atlantica	Chartered fisheries research vessel, 138, 238	
Galiano	Fisheries patrol vessel, 90	
Gannet	Northern supply vessel, 201	
Gauss	Antarctic exploration vessel, became *Arctic*, 30	
General Schmidlin	Became *Cedarwood*, 257	
Gen. U.S. Grant	Tug, ex *Edsall*, became *Bayfield (1)*, 97	
George E. Darby	Search and rescue cutter, 207	
George R. Pearkes	Light icebreaker and navigation aids tender, 176	
Givenchy	Fisheries patrol vessel, 91, 113	
Gladiator	Tug chartered for Customs patrol, 78	
Glenada	Survey vessel and tug, 270	
Glendon	Lighthouse supply vessel and buoy tender, 62	
Glenevis	Naval auxiliary tug, 143	
Gordon Reid	Search and rescue cutter, 134, 209	
Grenfell	Search and rescue cutter, 208	
Grenville (1)	Cook's survey schooner, 57, 94	
Grenville (2)	Lighthouse supply vessel and buoy tender, 94	
Grib	Customs patrol vessel, former whaler, 73	
Griffon	Light icebreaker and navigation aids tender, 174	
Gull Isle	Small buoy tender, 190	
Gulnare (1), (2) & (3)	Bayfield's survey schooners, 95	
Gulnare (4)	Fisheries patrol vessel, later a lightship, 87	
Harp	Search and rescue cutter, 210	
Heatherton	Naval Auxiliary tug, 267	
Hector	Whaler—became *Diana*, 29	
Henry Larsen	Icebreaker, 156	
Higgett	RCMP patrol vessel, 218	
Hildur	Motor yacht—became *Bayfield (3)*, 249	
Hood	Search and rescue cutter, 210	
Howay	Fisheries patrol vessel, formerly *Macdonald*, 142, 221	
Hudson	Hydrographic & oceanographic vessel, 139, 245	
Hudson Service	Offshore supply vessel, became *Mary Hichens*, 208	
Hunter Point	Fisheries patrol vessel—became *Rider*, 223	
Ile des Barques	Small buoy tender, 191	
Ile Rouge	Small search and rescue cutter, 211	
Ile Saint-Ours	Small buoy tender, 191	
Inkster	RCMP patrol vessel, 218	
Irvine	RCMP patrol vessel, 214	
Ivan Susanin	Soviet icebreaker, ex *Minto*, 36	
J.D. Hazen	Icebreaker, became *Mikula (1)*, 41	
J.E. Bernier	Light icebreaker and navigation aids tender, 174	
J.E. Kinney	Became *Cedarwood*, 257	
Jackman	Search and Rescue cutter, 208	
Jalobert	Tug, 111	
James Howden	Tug, 110	
James Sinclair	Fisheries patrol vessel, 227	
Janie B.	Offshore supply vessel, 207	
John A. Macdonald	Icebreaker, 122, 151	
John Cabot	Cable ship and icebreaker, 160	
John Jacobson	Search and rescue cutter, 209	
John P. Tully	Hydrographic/oceanographic vessel, 251	
Kalvik	Icebreaking supply ship, 158	
Kanada	Russian icebreaker, ex *Earl Grey (1)*, 40	
Kapuskasing	Hydrographic and Naval Auxiliary vessel, 242, 261	
Karluk	Northern exploration vessel, 31	
Kenoki	Navigation aids tender, 187	
Kestrel	Fisheries patrol vessel, 87	
King and Winge	American Schooner, 31	
King Edward	Trawler—became *Laurentian*, 67	
Kingfisher	Fisheries patrol schooner, 81	
Kurdistan	Tanker, 171	
La Canadienne (1)	Fisheries patrol schooner, 83	
La Canadienne (2)	Fisheries patrol, and survey vessel, 84, 101	
Labrador	Icebreaker, 150	

Labrador	Trawler—became *Bernier*, 68	
Lady Grey	Icebreaker, 39	
Lady Hammond	Chartered fisheries research vessel, 238	
Lady Head	Pre-confederation steamer, 23	
Lady Laurier	Lighthouse supply vessel and buoy tender, 51, 78	
Lake Como	Became *Beothic*, 114	
Lambton	Lighthouse supply vessel and buoy tender, 65	
Lamna	Formerly *Cygnus (2)*, 222	
Lansdowne	Lighthouse supply vessel and buoy tender, 47	
Lanoraie II	Survey and inspection vessel, 109	
Laurentian	Lighthouse supply vessel and buoy tender, 67, 78	
Laurier	RCMP and fisheries patrol vessel, 79, 221	
Laymore	Naval Auxiliary cargo vessel, 265	
Le Quebecois	Fisheries patrol vessel, 228	
Leebro	Chartered lighthouse supply vessel, 64	
Leonard J. Cowley	Fisheries patrol vessel, 227	
Lightship No. 1	(Sambro), 276	
Lightship No. 2	(Lurcher), 276	
Lightship No. 3	Formerly *Messines*, 113	
Lightship No. 5	Formerly *Vimy*, 113	
Lightship No. 7	Nineteenth century lightship, 113	
Lightship No. 20	Formerly *St. Eloi*, 113	
Lightship No. 22	Formerly *St. Julien*, 113	
Lillooet	Hydrographic survey vessel, 99	
Limnos	Great Lakes research vessel, 248	
Lindsay	RCMP patrol vessel, 218	
Lingan	Collier, 53	
Lisgar	DPW tug used for Customs patrol, 78	
Loos	Lighthouse supply vessel and buoy tender, 67, 113	
Lord Stanley	Tug, became *Bayfield (2)*, 98	
Lord Strathcona	Salvage vessel, 106	
Louis M. Lauzier	Oceanographic research vessel, ex *Cape Harrison*, 226, 250	
Louis S. St. Laurent	Icebreaker, 121, 152	
Louisbourg	Fisheries patrol vessel, 226	
Macassar	Tug formerly *Jalobert*, 111	
MacBrien	RCMP patrol vessel, 214	
Macdonald	RCMP patrol vessel—became *Howay*, 79	
Mackay Bennett	Cable ship, 53	
Magnificent	RCN Aircraft Carrier, 149	
Malaspina	Fisheries patrol vessel, 90	
Manhattan	American icebreaking tanker, 148, 151, 152	
Marabell	Hydrographic survey vessel—former USN minesweeper, 243	
Mardep	Trawler—became *Bernier*, 68	
Margaret	Customs patrol vessel, 72	
Marinus	Fisheries research vessel, 234	
Marmot	Northern supply landing craft, 200.	
Martha L. Black	Light icebreaker and navigation aids tender, 176	
Mary Hichens	Search and rescue cutter, 208	
Matthew	Hydrographic& oceanographic vessel, 253	
Maxwell	Hydrographic survey vessel, 246	
Mayita	Steam yacht chartered for Customs patrol, 78	
Melville	RCN minesweeper—became *Cygnus (1)*, 220	
Merrickville	Naval auxiliary tug, 143	
Messines	Naval trawler, converted to lightship, 113	
Mikula (1)	Icebreaker, formerly *J.D. Hazen*, 41	
Mikula (2)	Training ship, formerly Lightship No.4, 274	
Mikula Seleaninovitch	Russian icebreaker, formerly *J.D. Hazen*, 41	
Mink	Northern supply landing craft, 200	
Minto	Icebreaker, 36	
Miskinaw	Special river navigation aids tender, 193	
Montcalm (1)	Icebreaker, 37	
Montcalm (2)	Light icebreaker and navigation aids tender, 168	
Montmagny (1)	Lighthouse supply vessel and buoy tender, 53	
Montmagny (2)	Navigation aids tender, 186	
Montmorency	Ice-strengthened navigation aids vessel, 178	
Murray Stewart	Tug, 110	
N.B. McLean	Icebreaker, 43, 126	
Nadon	RCMP patrol vessel, 218	
Nahidik	Special river buoy tender, 196	
Namao	Buoy tender on Lake Winnipeg, 189	
Nanook	Northern depot ship, 202	
Napoleon III	Pre-confederation steamer, 21	
Narwhal	Depot ship and navigation aids tender, 173	

Nascopie	Hudson Bay Company icebreaker and supply vessel, 30, 115	
Neptune	Northern exploration vessel, 27	
New Liskeard	Naval Auxiliary research vessel, 261	
Newfield	Lighthouse supply vessel and buoy tender, 46	
Newington	Lighthouse supply vessel and buoy tender, 64	
Nicolet	Sounding vessel, 272	
Niobe	RCN cruiser, 51	
Norman McLeod Rogers	Icebreaker, 153	
North Star IV	Chartered survey vessel, 239	
Northern Light	Early icebreaker, 27, 34	
Northwind	USCG icebreaker, 151	
Ocean Eagle	Tug, 112	
Oshawa	Naval Auxiliary research vessel, 261	
Parizeau	Hydrographic & oceanographic vessel, 247	
Parry	Small hydrographic survey vessel, 241	
Partridge Island	Small buoy tender, 191	
Pathfinder	Steam yacht, became *Conestoga*, 74	
Patrol Boat No. IV	Customs patrol vessel, former rum runner, 73	
Pelican	Fisheries patrol vessel, ex RN sloop, 85	
Pembroke	Royal Navy ship, 92	
Petrel	Fisheries patrol vessel, 86	
Pierre Radisson	Icebreaker, 124, 154	
Pisces III	Submersible, 159, 160	
Point Henry	Small search and rescue cutter, 211	
Point Race	Small search and rescue cutter, 211	
Polana	Tug—became *Jalobert*, 111	
POLAR 8	Projected icebreaker, 157	
Polar Sea	USCG icebreaker, 151, 152	
Ponvert	American brig, 21	
Porte Dauphine	Survey vessel, 270	
Preventor	Customs and RCMP patrol vessel, 76	
Princess	Lighthouse supply vessel and buoy tender, 52	
Princess Louise	Lighthouse supply vessel, lost incomplete, 47	
Provo Wallis	Ice-strengthened navigation aids vessel, 182	
Puffin	Northern supply vessel, 201	
Quadra (1)	Lighthouse supply vessel and buoy tender, 24, 48	
Quadra (2)	Weather ship, 130, 164	
Queen City	Tug—formerly *Jalobert*, 111	
Queen Victoria	Pre-confederation steamer, 18, 21	
Quest	Naval Auxiliary research vessel, 263	
R.B. Young	Hydrographic & oceanographic vessel, 253	
Racer	Search and rescue cutter, 205	
Rally	Search and rescue cutter, 205	
Rapid	Search and rescue cutter, 205	
Raven	Northern supply vessel, 201	
Ready	Search and rescue cutter, 205	
Relay	Search and rescue cutter, 205	
Restless	Steam yacht chartered for Customs, 78	
Richelieu	Pre-confederation steamer, 19	
Rider	Search and rescue cutter, 205	
Riverton (1)	Naval Auxiliary tug, 267	
Riverton (2)	Naval Auxiliary vessel, 264	
Robert Foulis	Small buoy tender, 188	
Roosevelt	Peary's exploration ship, 31	
Rouville	Lighthouse supply vessel and buoy tender, 63	
Sackville	Naval Auxiliary research vessel, 259	
Safeguard	Became *Safeguarder*, 58	
Safeguarder	Lighthouse supply vessel and buoy tender, 58	
Sagamore	Steam yacht chartered for Customs patrol, 78	
Saint Anthony	Naval Auxiliary tug, 267	
Saint Charles	Naval Auxiliary tug, 267	
Saint John	Naval Auxiliary tug, 267	
Samuel Risley	Light icebreaker and navigation aids tender, 175	
Saurel	Icebreaker, 42	
Savannah	Nuclear powered freighter, 152	
Scarab II	Cable burying robot vehicle, 160	
Scatari	Customs Patrol vessel, former rum runner, 74	
Scout	Small buoy tender, 63	
Shamook	Fisheries research vessel, 234	
Shamrock	Small buoy tender, 62	
Simcoe (1)	Lighthouse supply vessel and buoy tender, 54	
Simcoe (2)	Ice-strengthened navigation aids vessel, 181	
Simmonds	RCMP patrol vessel, 218	

Simon Fraser	Ice-strengthened navigation aids vessel, 179	
Sipu-Muin	Hovercraft, 280	
Sir Humphrey Gilbert	Light icebreaker and navigation aids tender, 169	
Sir James Douglas (1)	Pre-confederation steamer, 24	
Sir James Douglas (2)	Navigation aids tender, 184	
Sir John Franklin	Icebreaker, originally *Franklin (2)*, 154	
Sir Wilfred Grenfell	Search and rescue cutter, 209	
Sir Wilfrid Laurier	Light icebreaker and navigation aids tender, 176	
Sir William Alexander (1)	Light icebreaker and navigation aids tender, 171	
Sir William Alexander (2)	Light icebreaker and navigation aids tender, 177	
Siyäy	Hovercraft, 136, 280	
Skidegate	Small buoy tender, 188	
Skua	Northern supply vessel, 127, 201	
Speedy II	D.P.W. survey vessel, 101	
Spindrift	Small search and rescue cutter, 211	
Spray	Small search and rescue cutter, 211	
Spume	Small search and rescue cutter, 211	
St. Arvans	Tug—became *Ocean Eagle*, 112	
St. Catharines	Weather ship, 162	
St. Eloi	Naval trawler, converted to lightship, 113	
St. Finbarr	Became *Franklin (1)*, 60	
St. Heliers	Lighthouse supply vessel and buoy tender, 59	
St. Julien	Naval trawler, converted to lightship, 113	
St. Roch	RCMP Northern exploration vessel, 32	
St. Roch II	Temporary name of RCMP *Nadon*, 218	
St. Stephen	Weather ship, 163	
Stadacona	Hydrographic survey and fisheries patrol vessel, 103	
Stanley	Icebreaker, 35, 78	
Stone Town	Weather ship, 163	
Stumble Inn	Rum runner—became *Patrol Boat No.IV*, 73	
Sultana	Eighteenth century schooner, 94	
Talapus	Fishing vessel—became *Parry*, 241	
Tanu	Fisheries patrol vessel, 224	
Teleost	Fisheries research vessel, 237	
Tembah	Special river navigation aids tender, 195	
Terra Nova	Chartered survey vessel, 239	
Terry Fox	Icebreaking supply ship, 158	
Thomas Carleton	Ice-strengthened navigation aids vessel., 180	
Tillicum	Motor yacht—became *Bayhound*, 75	
Titanic	Lost White Star liner, 53	
Tracy	Ice-strengthened navigation aids vessel, 181	
Traverse	Salvage vessel, 106	
Tsekoa II	Small buoy tender, 189	
Tupper	Ice-strengthened navigation aids vessel, 179	
Ulna	RCMP patrol vessel, former yacht, 78	
Ungava	Chartered northern patrol vessel, 30, 114	
Vancouver	Weather ship, 164	
Vector	Hydrographic survey vessel, 246	
Verendrye	Navigation aids tender, 128, 185	
Vicca	Motor yacht—became *Bayfield (3)*, 249	
Victoria	Schooner chartered for Customs patrol, 78	
Victoria	RCMP patrol vessel, 216	
Vigilant (1)	Fisheries patrol schooner, 78, 81	
Vigilant (2)	Fisheries patrol vessel, 88	
Ville Marie	Survey vessel and search and rescue cutter, 131, 271	
Vimy	Naval trawler, converted to lightship, 113	
Voyageur	Hovercraft, 137, 279	
W. Jackman	Self righting lifeboat, 212	
W.E. Ricker	Fisheries research vessel, 234	
W.G. George	Self righting lifeboat, 212	
Waban-aki	Hovercraft, 279	
Walter E. Foster	Ice-strengthened navigation aids vessel, 167	
Westwind	USCG icebreaker, 159	
Whitethroat	Naval Auxiliary vessel, 258	
Wilfred Templeman	Fisheries research vessel, 235	
William	Formerly *Sir William Alexander (1)*, 171	
Wm. J. Stewart	Hydrographic survey vessel, 104, 140	
Wolfe	Light icebreaker and navigation aids tender, 168	
Wood	RCMP patrol vessel—became *Daring*, 142, 217	
Woodstock	RCN corvette & weather ship, 161	
Yamal	Russian nuclear powered icebreaker, 152	
YMS 91	USN minesweeper—became *Marabell*, 243	
Yosemite	Became *Acadia (1)*, 84	

LIST OF SOURCES

Annual Publications

List of Ships Registered in Canada

Lloyd's Register of Shipping

Jane's Fighting Ships

Sessional Papers, Parliament of Canada

Books

Appleton, Thomas E. *Usque ad Mare: A History of the Canadian Coast Guard and Marine Services*. Ottawa: Department of Transport, 1968.

Delgado, James P. *Dauntless St. Roch, the Mounties Arctic Schooner*. Victoria: Horsdale & Schubart Publishers Ltd, 1992.

Elliot-Miesel, Elizabeth B. *Arctic Diplomacy: Canada and the United States in the Northwest Passage*. New York: Peter Lang Publishing Inc., 1998.

Fillmore, Stanley and R.W. Sandilands. *The Chartmakers*. Vancouver: NC Press Ltd and Canadian Hydrographic Service, 1983.

Freeman, David J. *Canadian Warship Names*. St. Catharines: Vanwell Publishing Ltd, 2000.

Frank, Alain. *Le Ernest Lapointe: Brise-Glace du Saint-Laurent*. L'Islet-sur-Mer: Musée Maritime Bernier, 1995.

Johnstone, Kenneth. *The Aquatic Explorers: A History of the Fisheries Research Board of Canada*. Toronto: University of Toronto Press & Ministry of Supply and Services, 1977.

Macpherson, Ken & John Burgess. *The Ships of Canada's Naval Forces 1910-1993*. St. Catharines: Vanwell Publishing Ltd, 1994.

Marcil, Eileen Reid. *Tall Ships and Tankers: The History of Davie Shipbuilders*. Toronto: McLelland & Stewart, 1997.

Mills, John M. *The New Mills List: Canadian Coastal and Inland Steam Vessels, 1809-1930*. Kingston: Marine Museum of the Great Lakes, 1999.

Milner, Marc. *HMCS Sackville 1941-1985*. Halifax: Canadian Naval Memorial Trust, 1998.

Niven, Jennifer. *The Ice Master: The Doomed 1913 Voyage of the Karluk*. New York: Hyperion, 2000.

Wild, Roland. *Arctic Command: The Story of Smellie of the Nascopie*. Toronto: Ryerson Press, 1955.

Other Documents and periodicals

Smith, Gordon W. *Icebreakers and Icebreaking in Canadian Arctic Waters*. Ottawa, 1990.

Technical and Operational Services, Canadian Coast Guard (D. Trudeau). *Ships of the Canadian Coast Guard*. Fisheries and Oceans Canada, 1999.

The DOT, Transport Canada, *Transpo 78, 79*, etc., *Fleet News, Echo*. (DOT and DFO in-house magazines).

The Island Magazine. Prince Edward Island Museum and Heritage Foundation.

THE AUTHORS

CHARLES DOUGLAS MAGINLEY who now lives in Mahone Bay, Nova Scotia, was born in Antigua in the West Indies in 1929. He sailed in cargo and passenger ships for eight years before joining the Royal Canadian Navy in 1955. On retiring from the Navy in 1976 he joined the Coast Guard as a Marine Surveyor and later taught at the Canadian Coast Guard College at Sydney, NS. He retired in 1990 but has kept in touch with maritime affairs and pursued a continuing interest in nautical history. He has been a frequent contributor to nautical history periodicals but this is his first book. Another, on the history of the Canadian Coast Guard, is in preparation.

BERNARD COLLIN was born in Montreal, Quebec in 1955. He has worked in the Canadian Coast Guard for 18 years, 12 at sea and the remainder in staff positions in the Coast Guard Headquarters in Ottawa. Bernard's interest in the history of the Canadian Coast Guard and Canadian Government ships has resulted in a vast personal collection of historical photographs and other archival material on ships dating back 150 years. The compilation of this collection has resulted from exhaustive and painstaking research through museums, federal and provincial government archives and private collections.